I Don't Know What I'm Doing

A Collection of Illustrations

By Richard "Doser" Almarez

Just an Introduction

The title says it all, I really don't know what I'm doing and upon the request of so many of you, I have finally decided to create this coloring book full of fun and imaginative houses as well as some other what's it who's its. This book was made for all of you so have fun with it! Color in it or don't (I'd prefer if you did). Thank you for all of the love and support! I hope you enjoy this book as much as I did making it!

-Richard

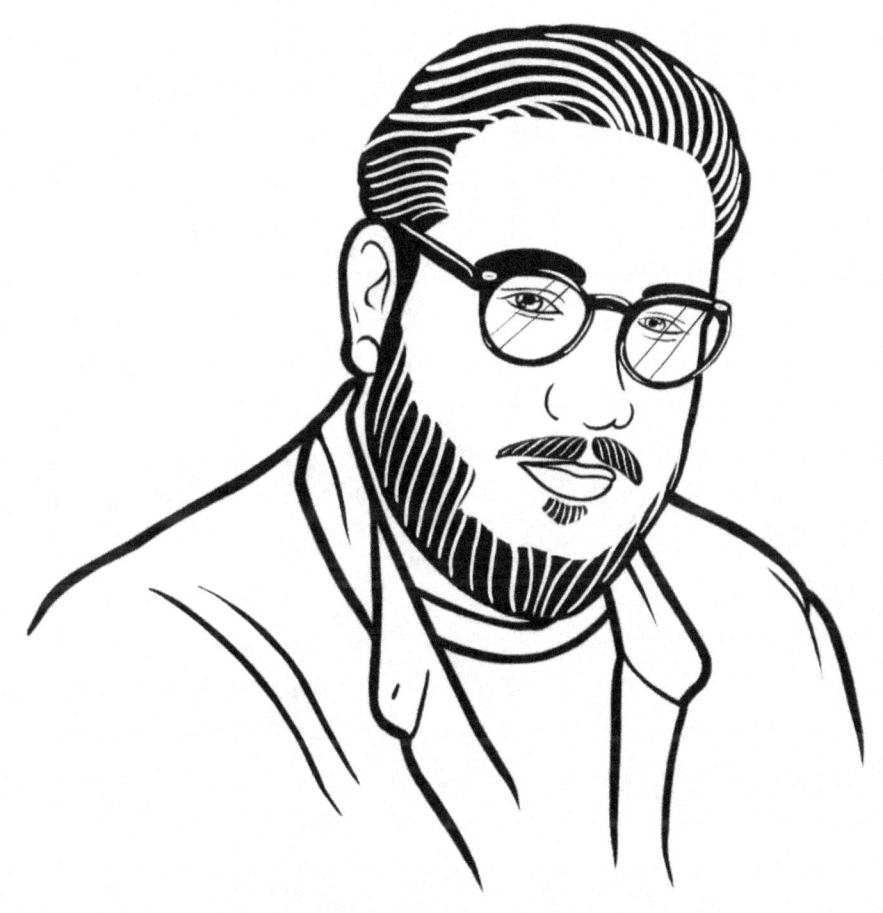

For Nico

"You will always be our dad"

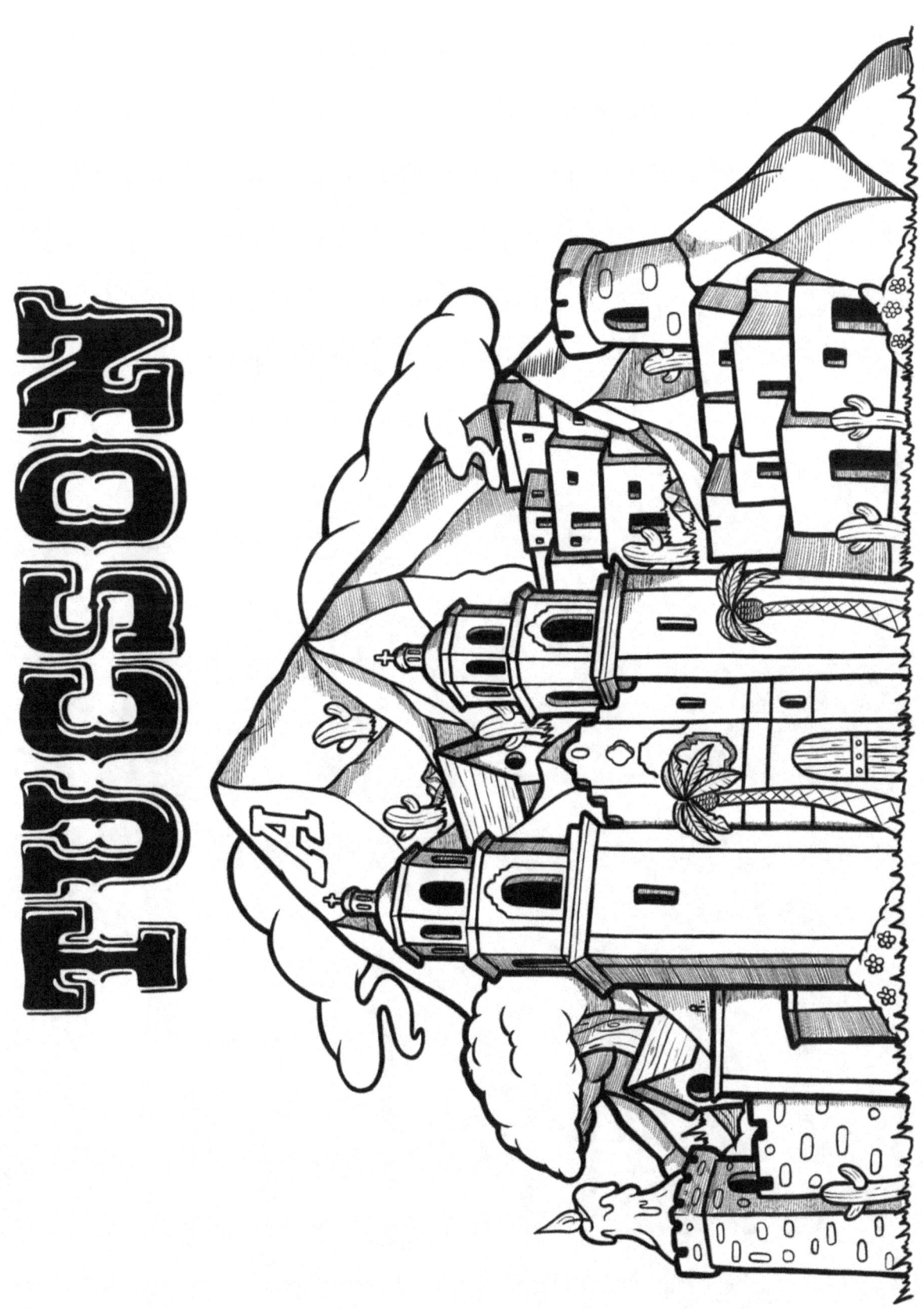

TUCSON

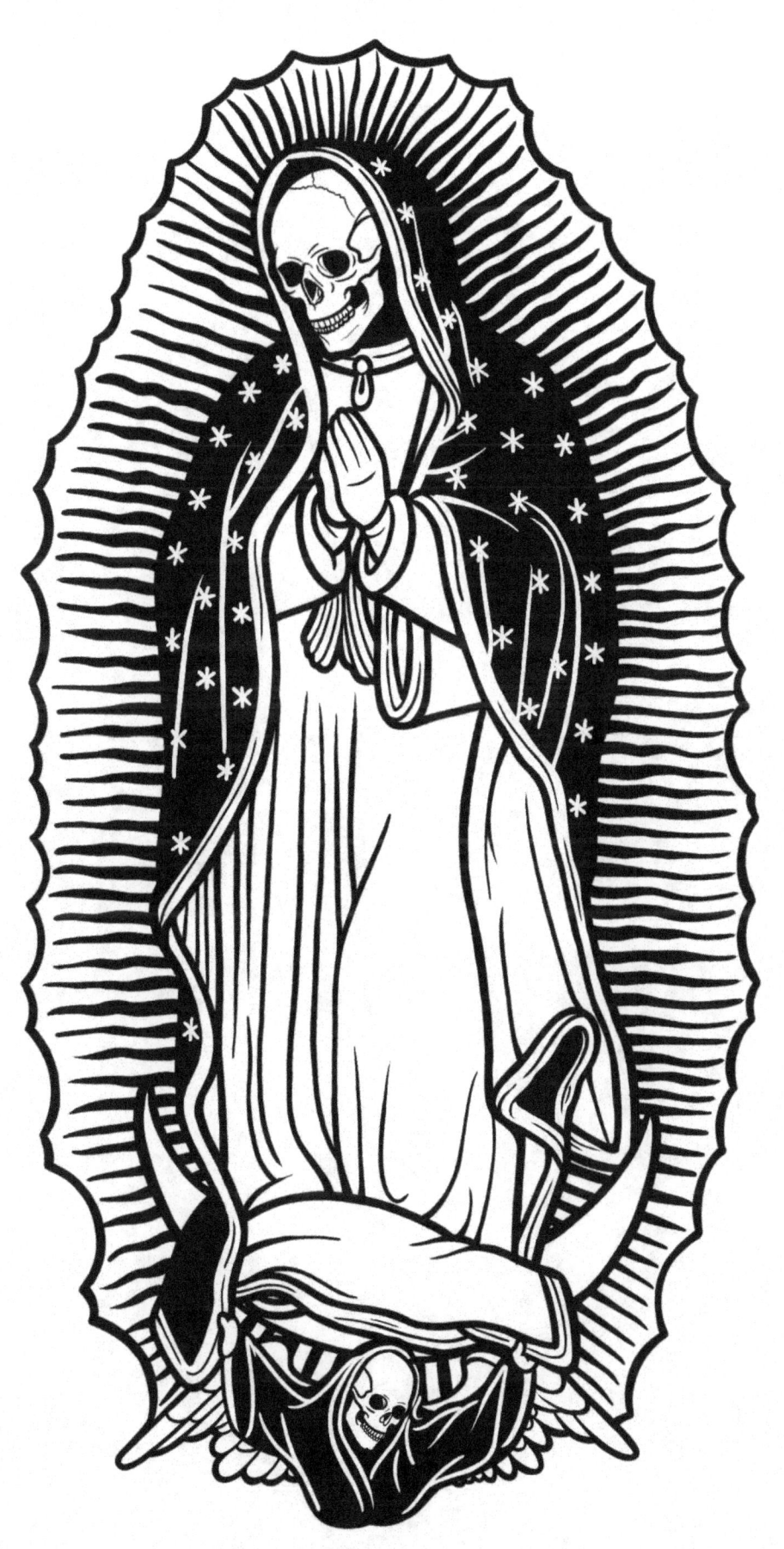

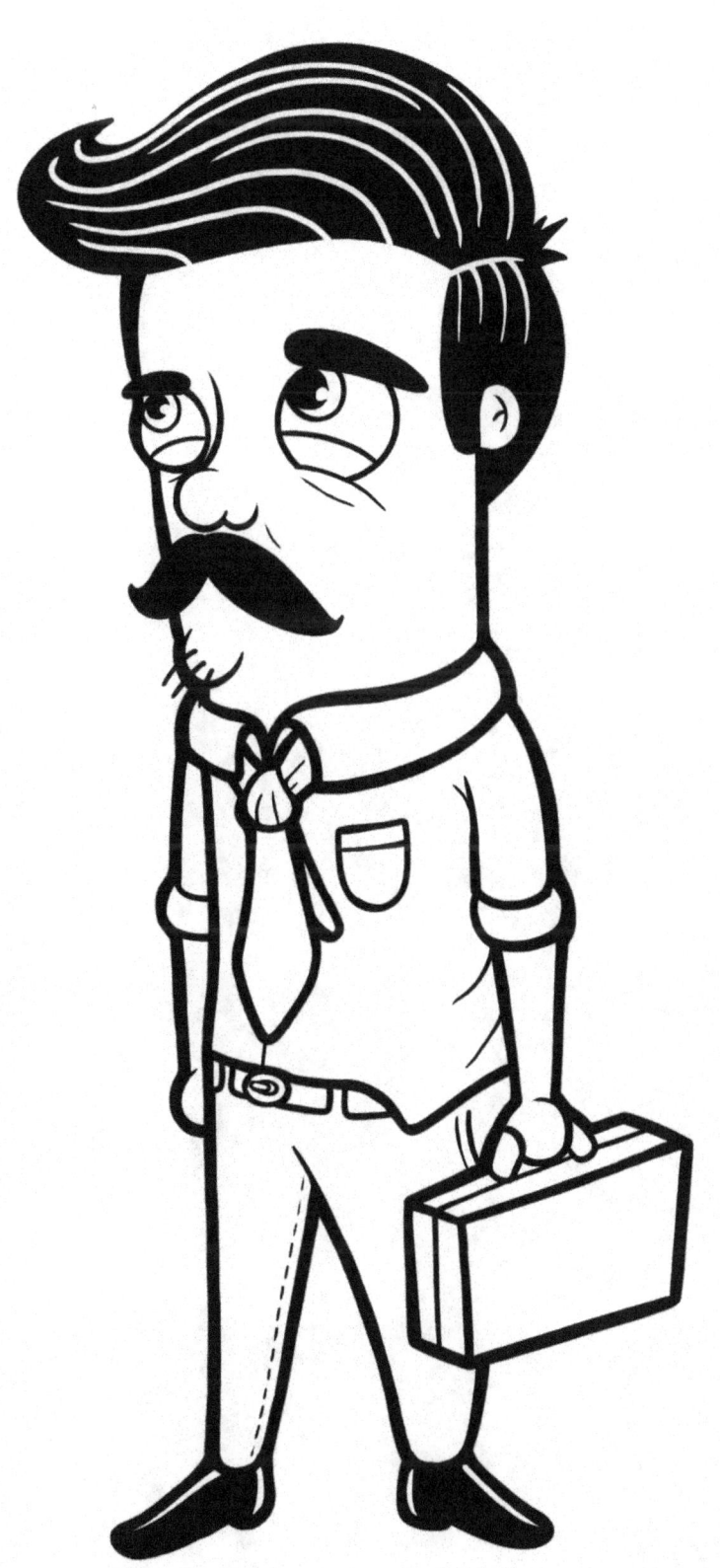

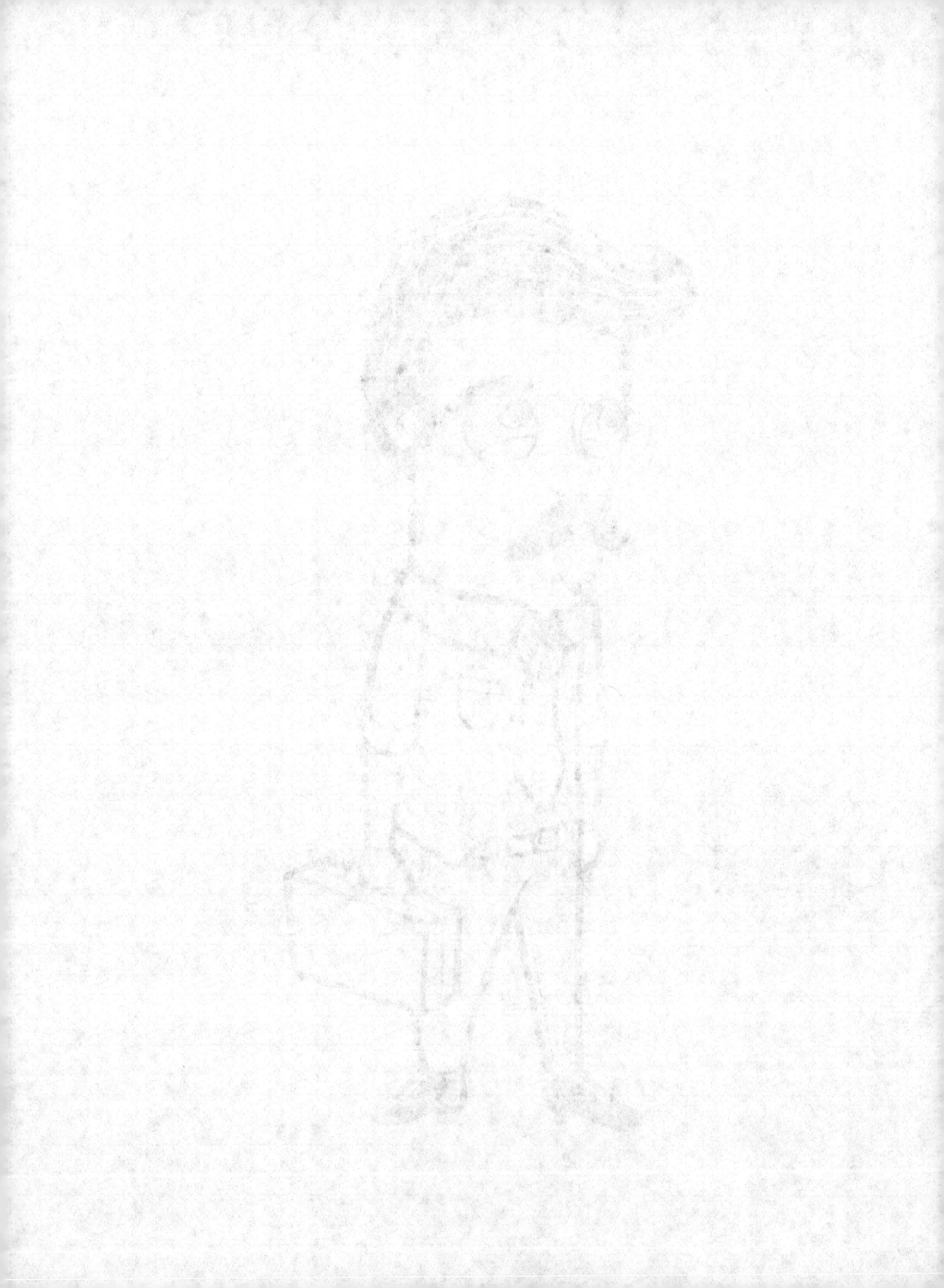

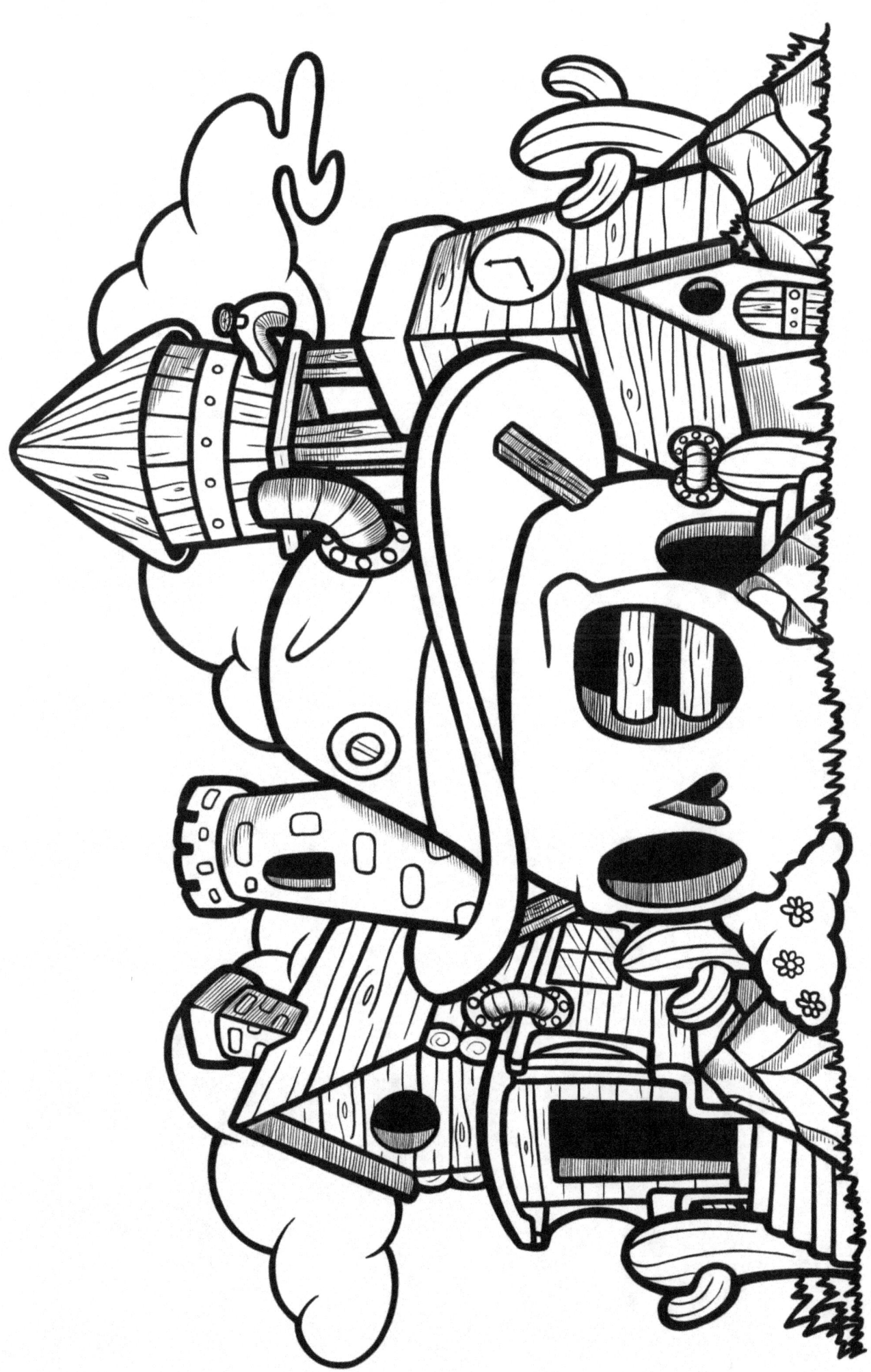

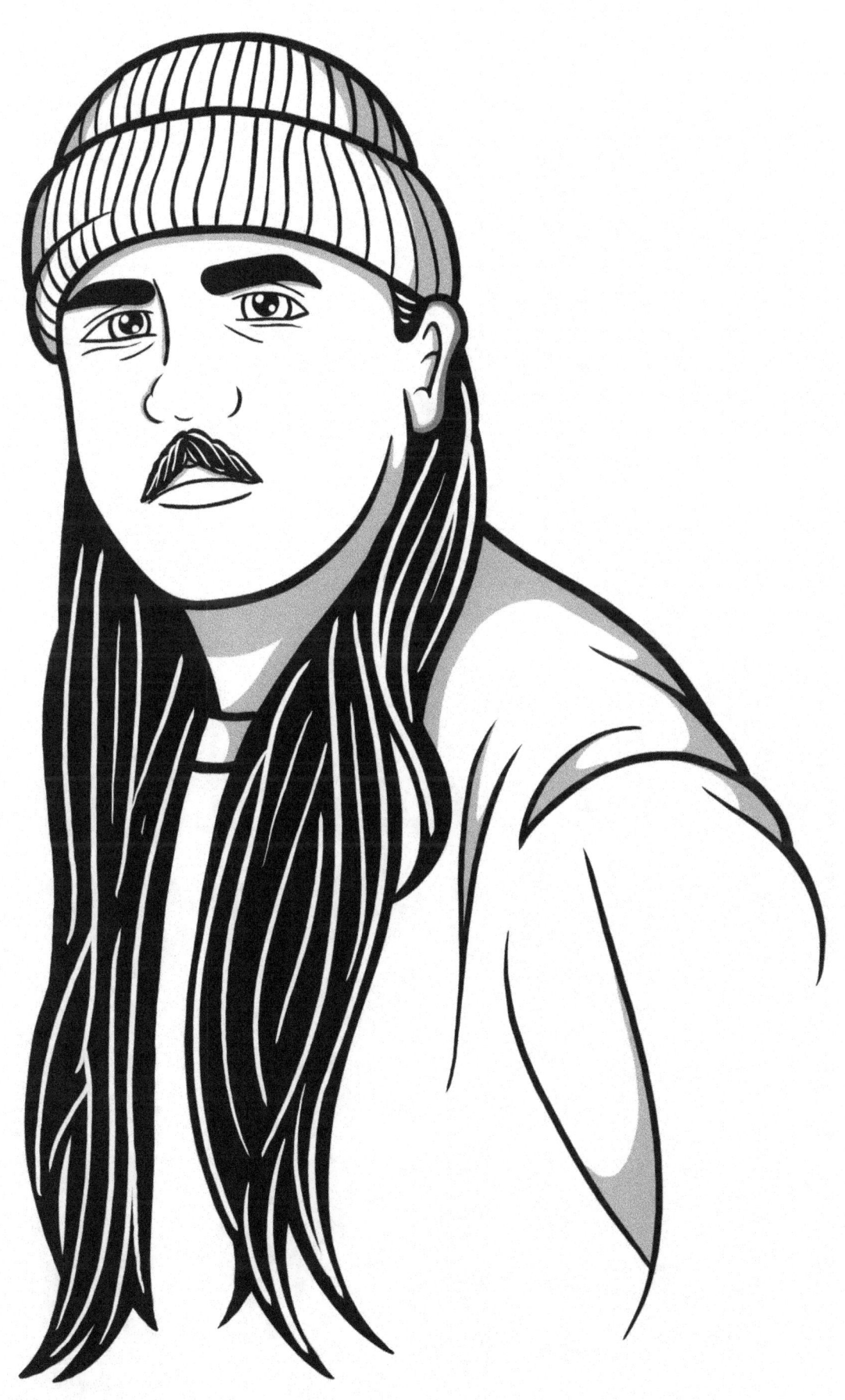

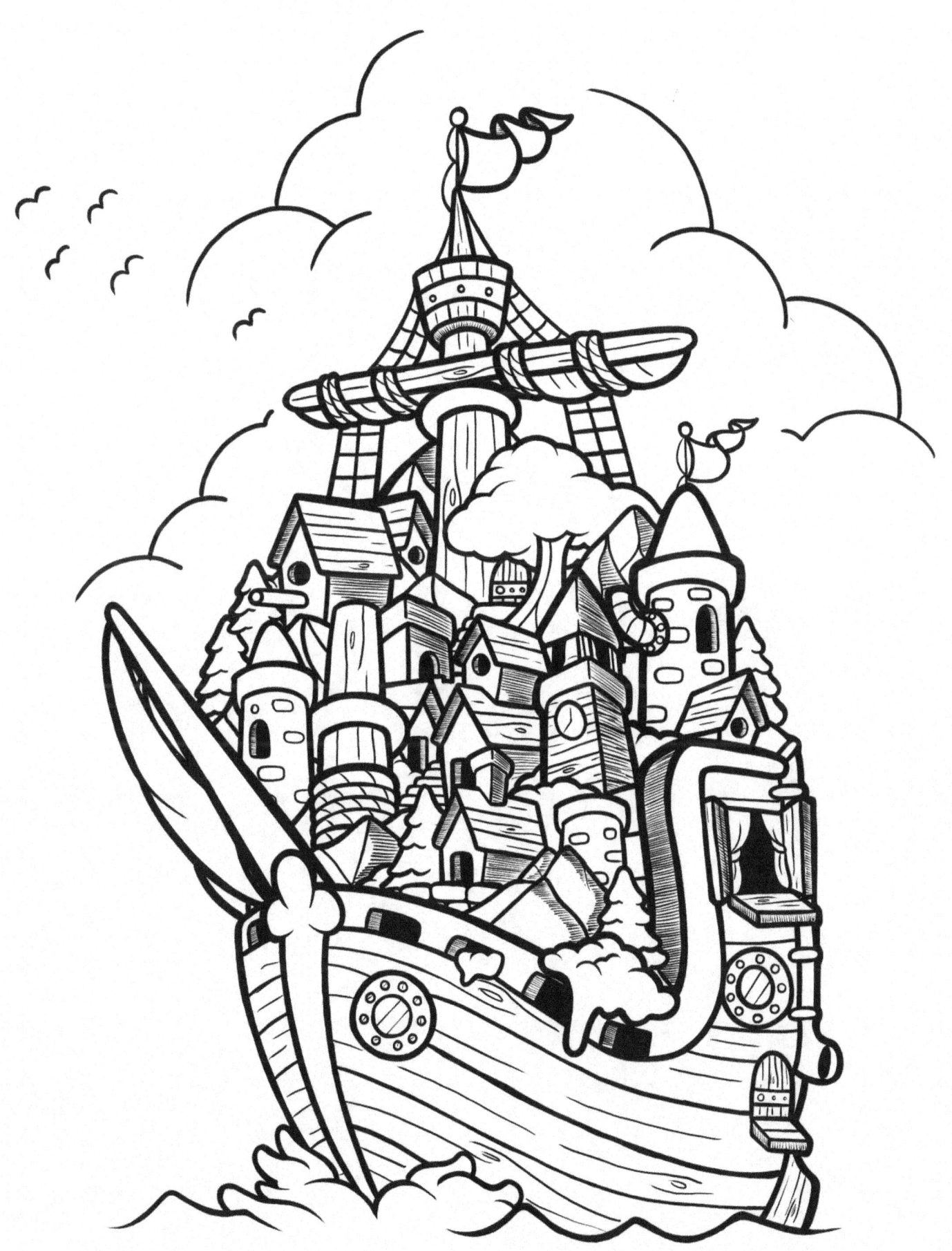

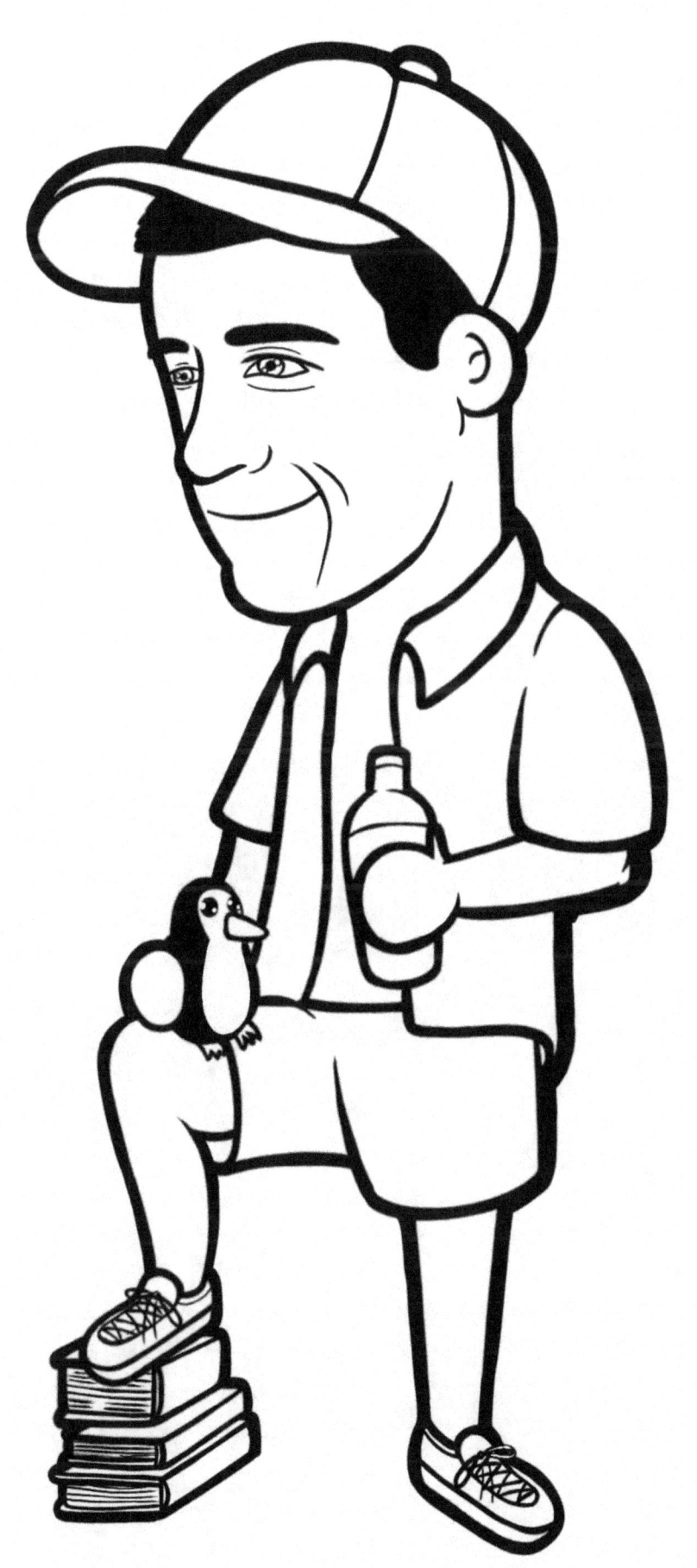

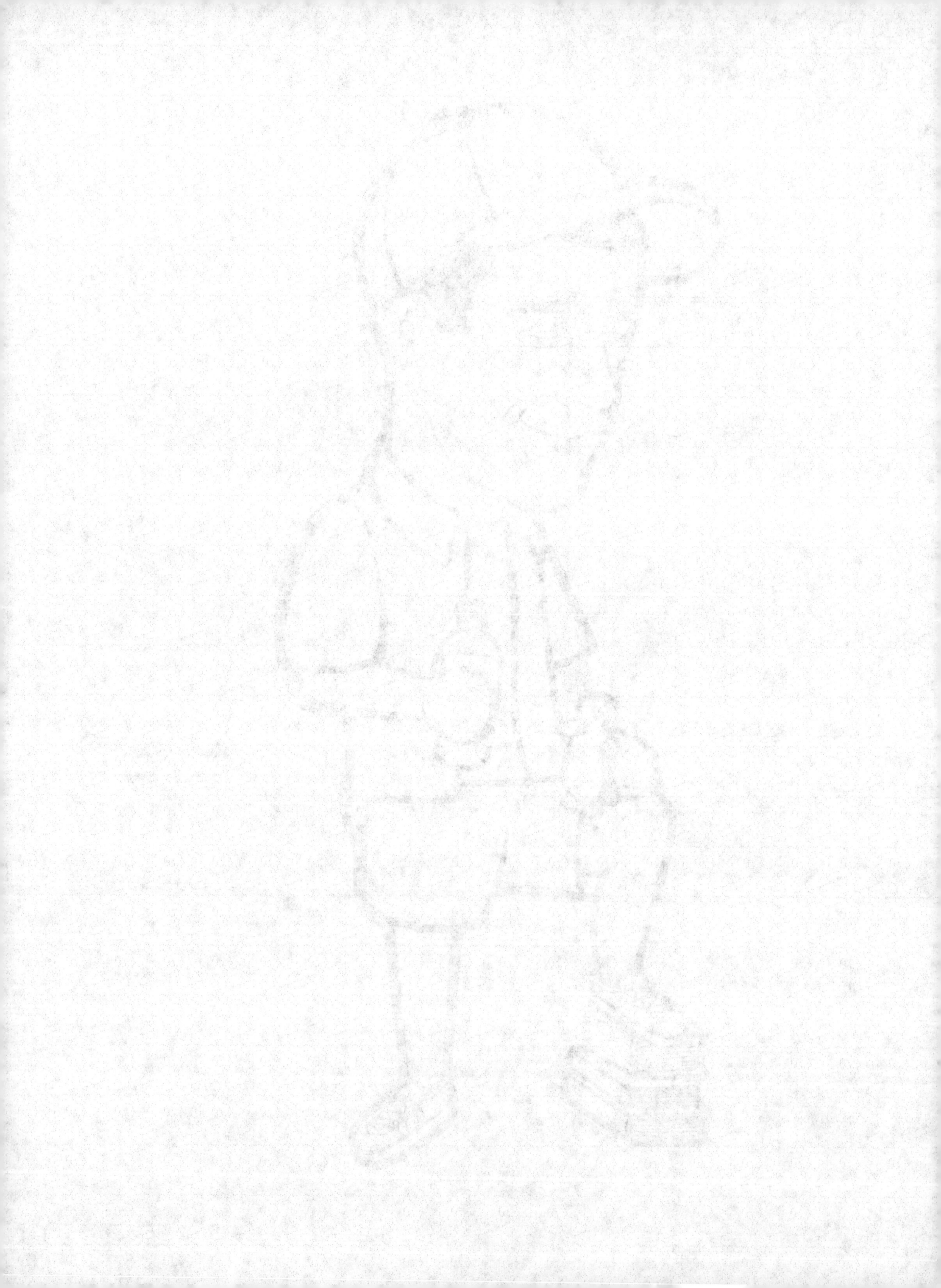

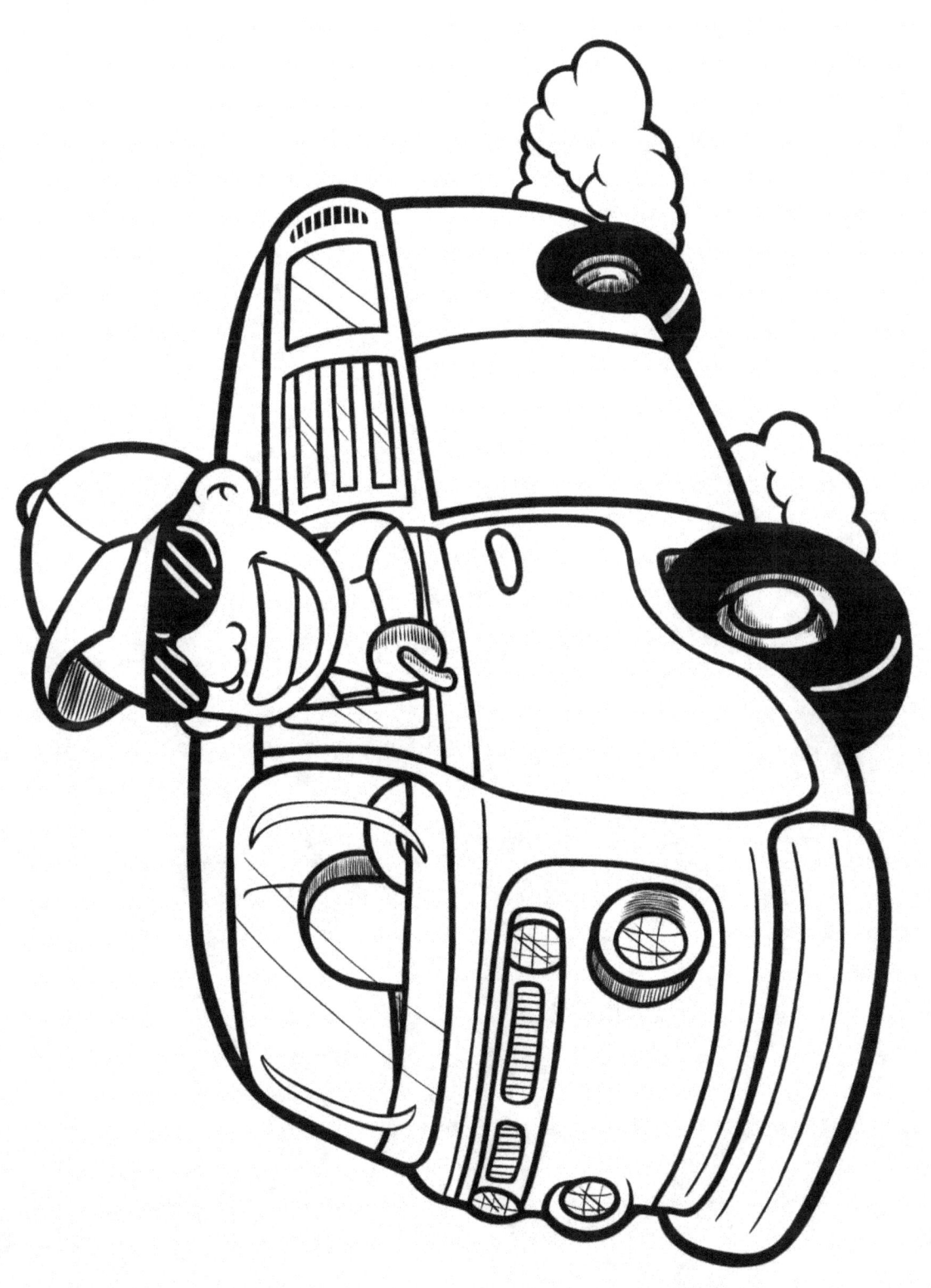

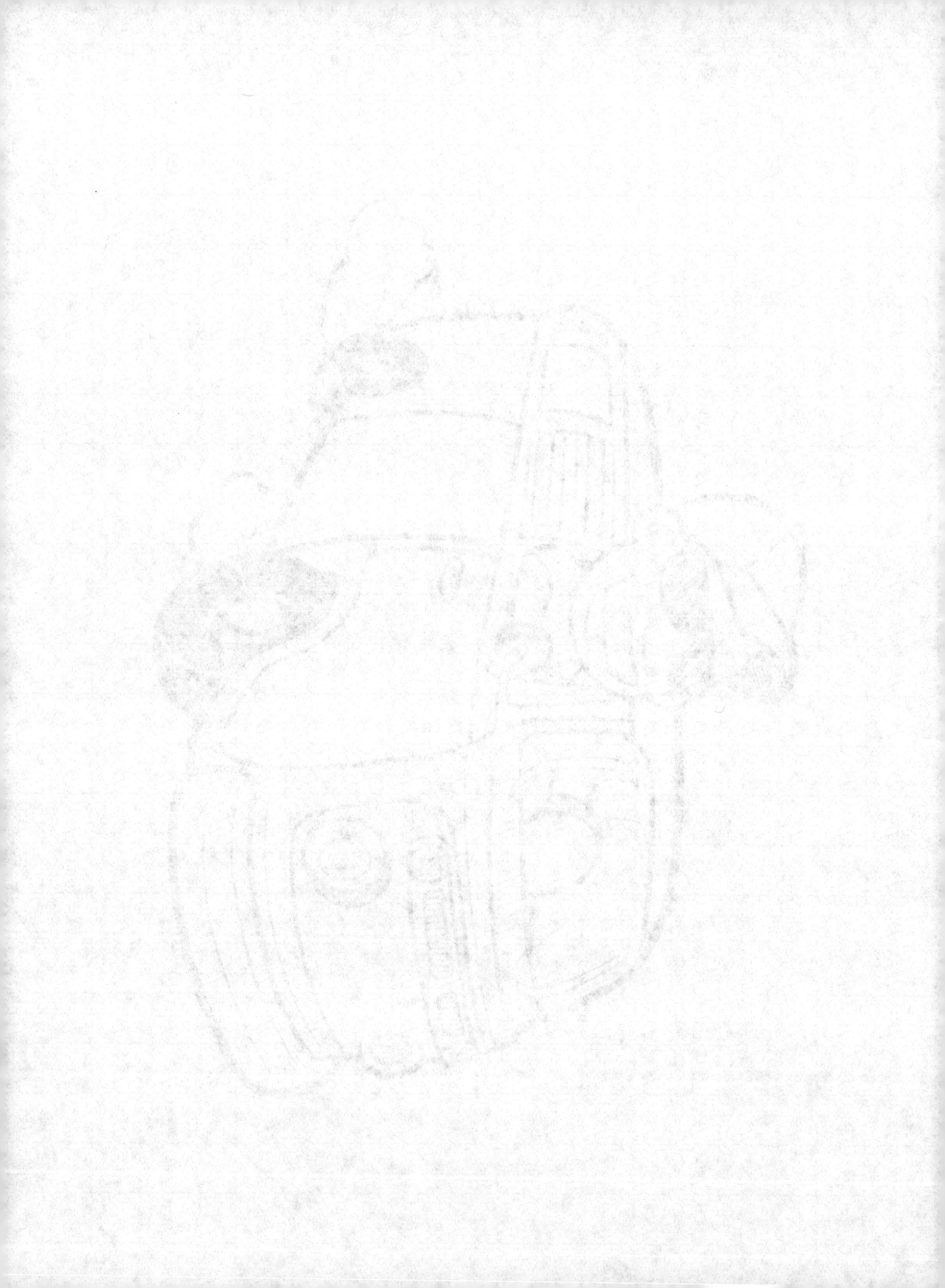

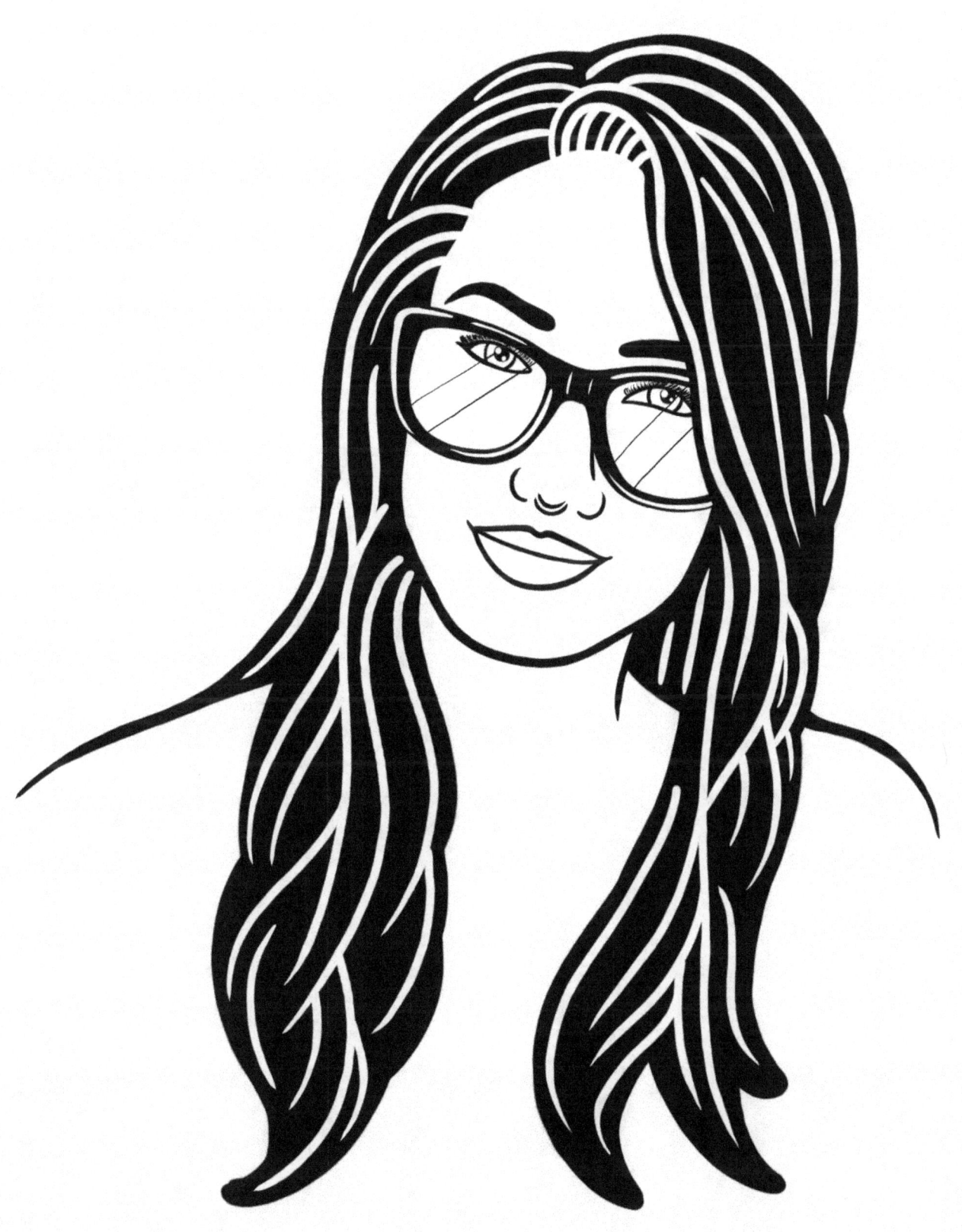

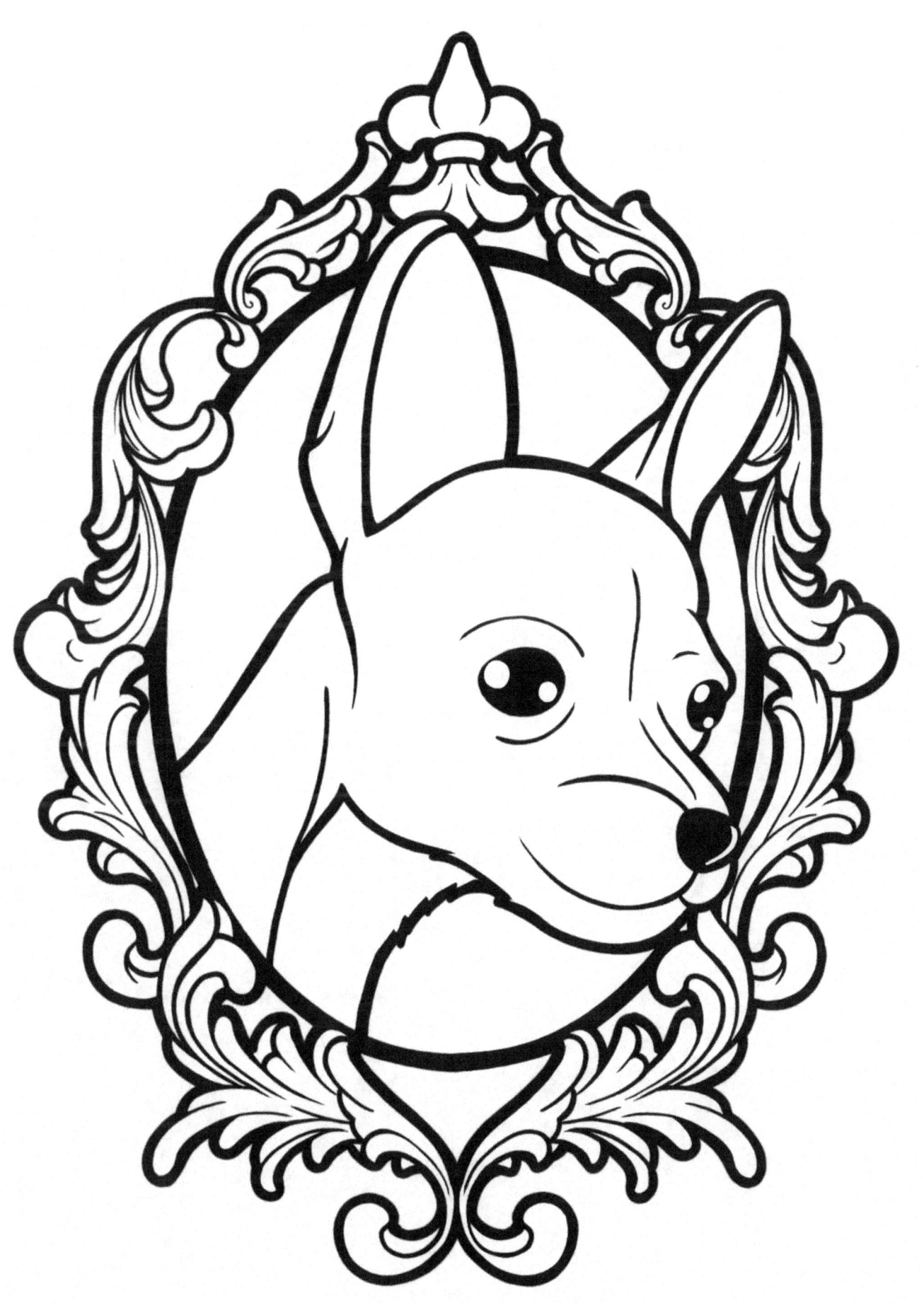

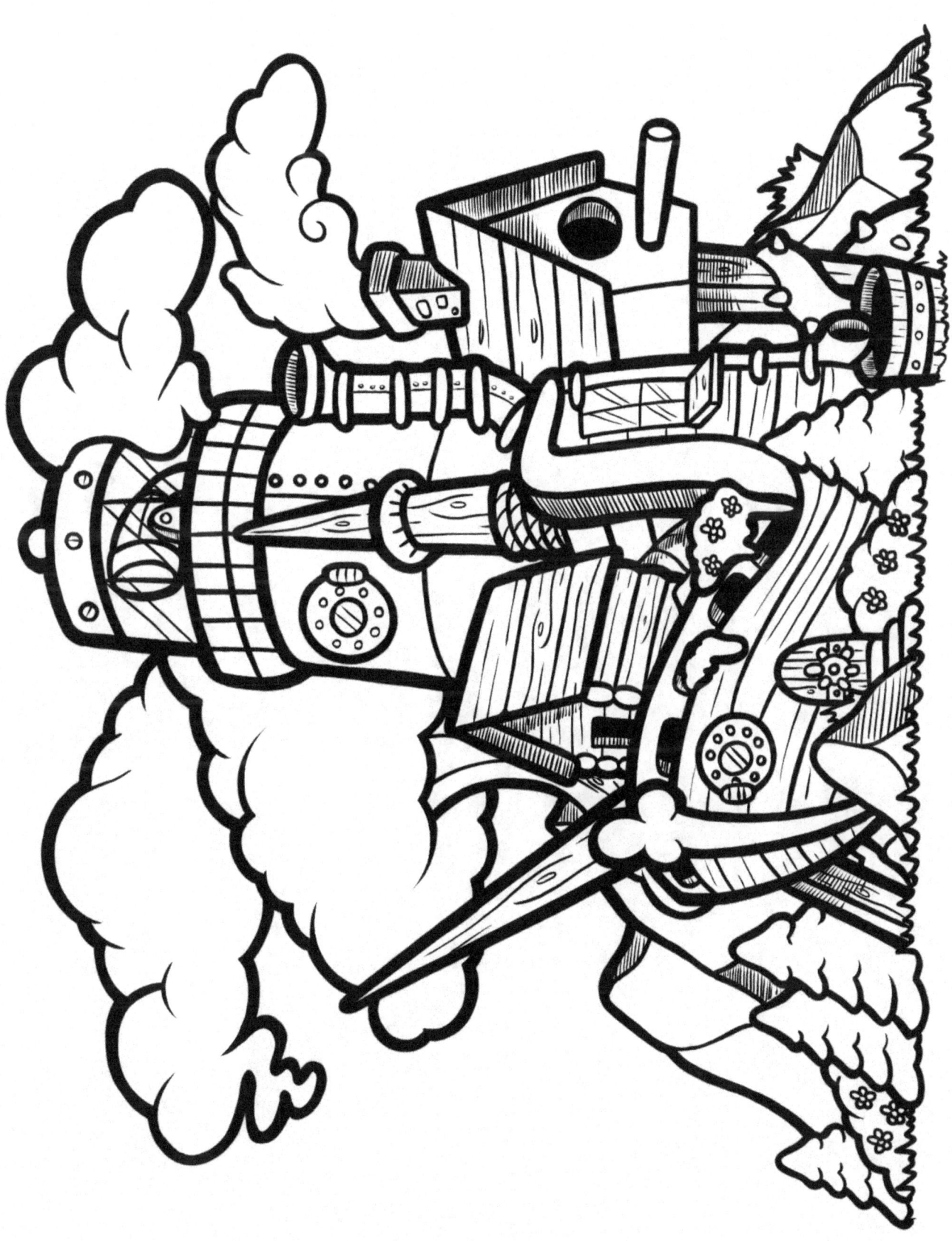

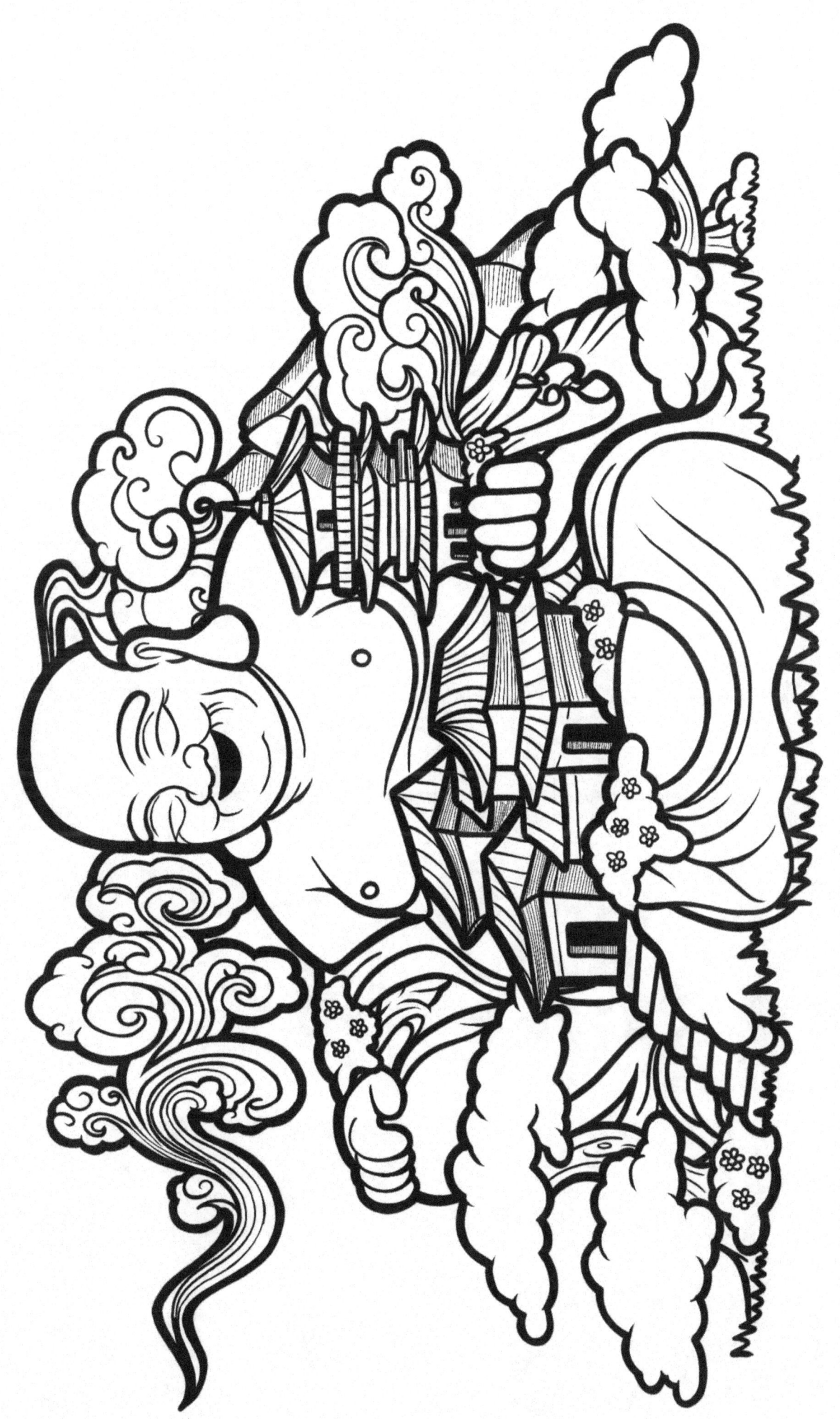

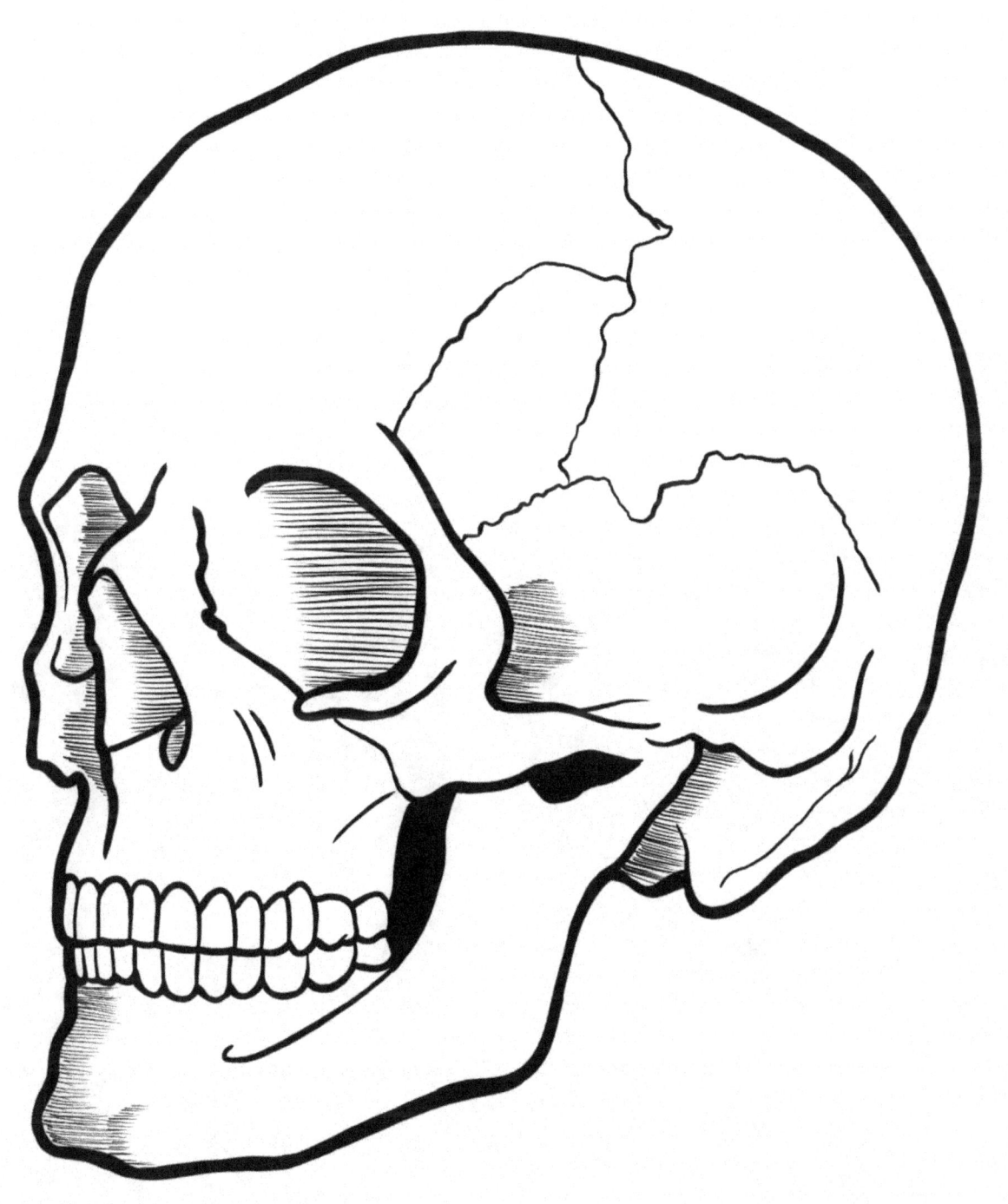

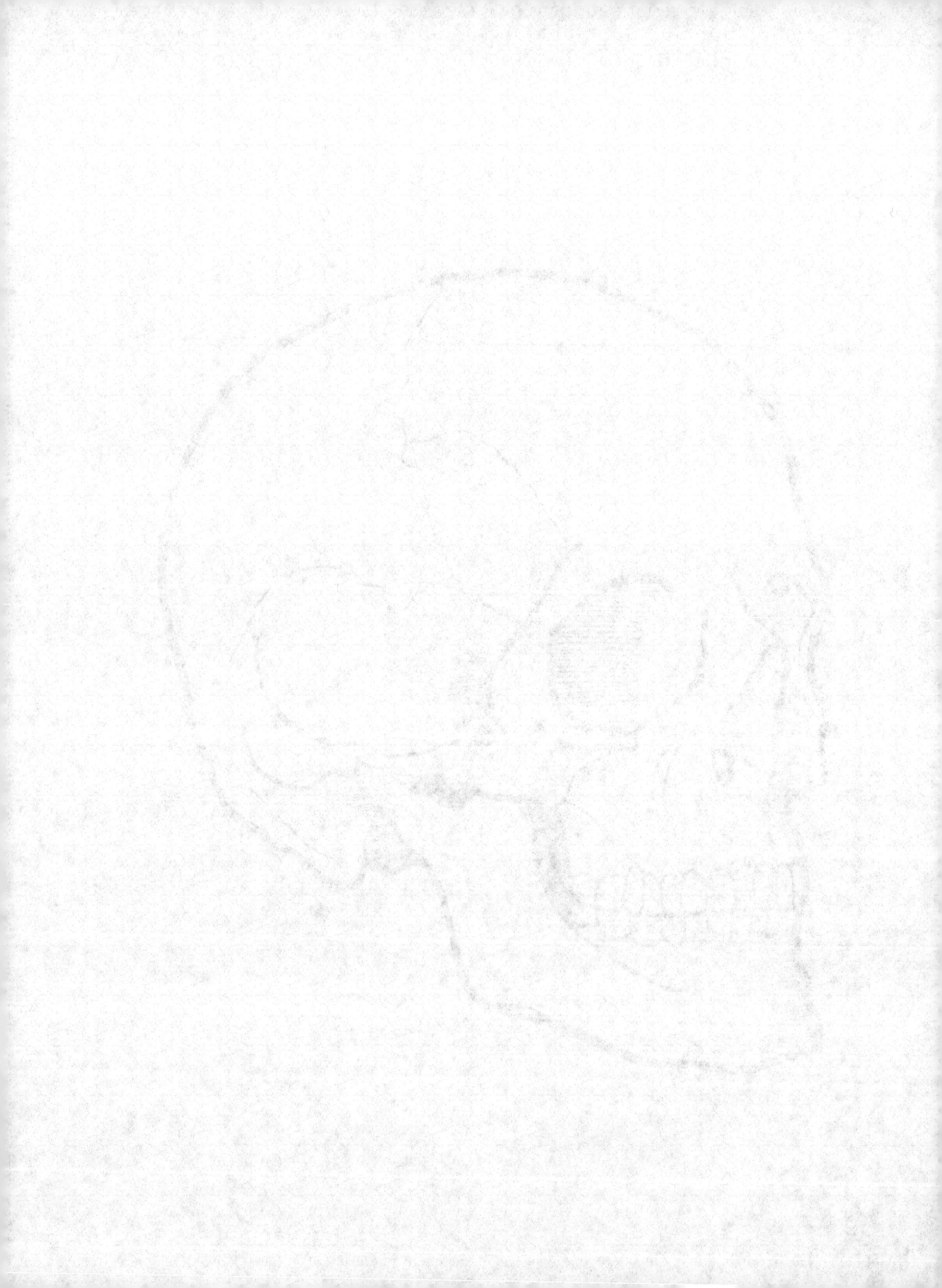

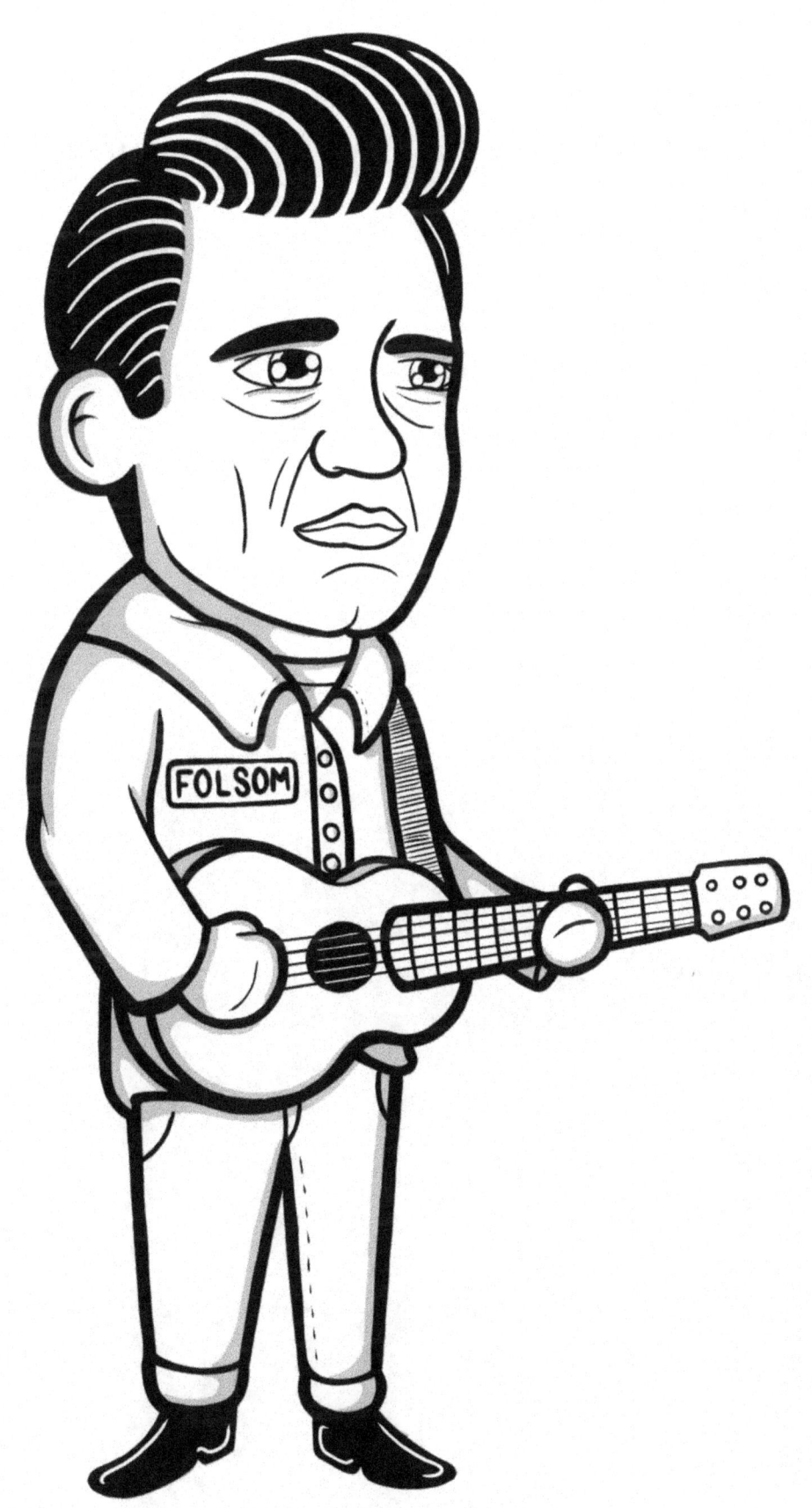

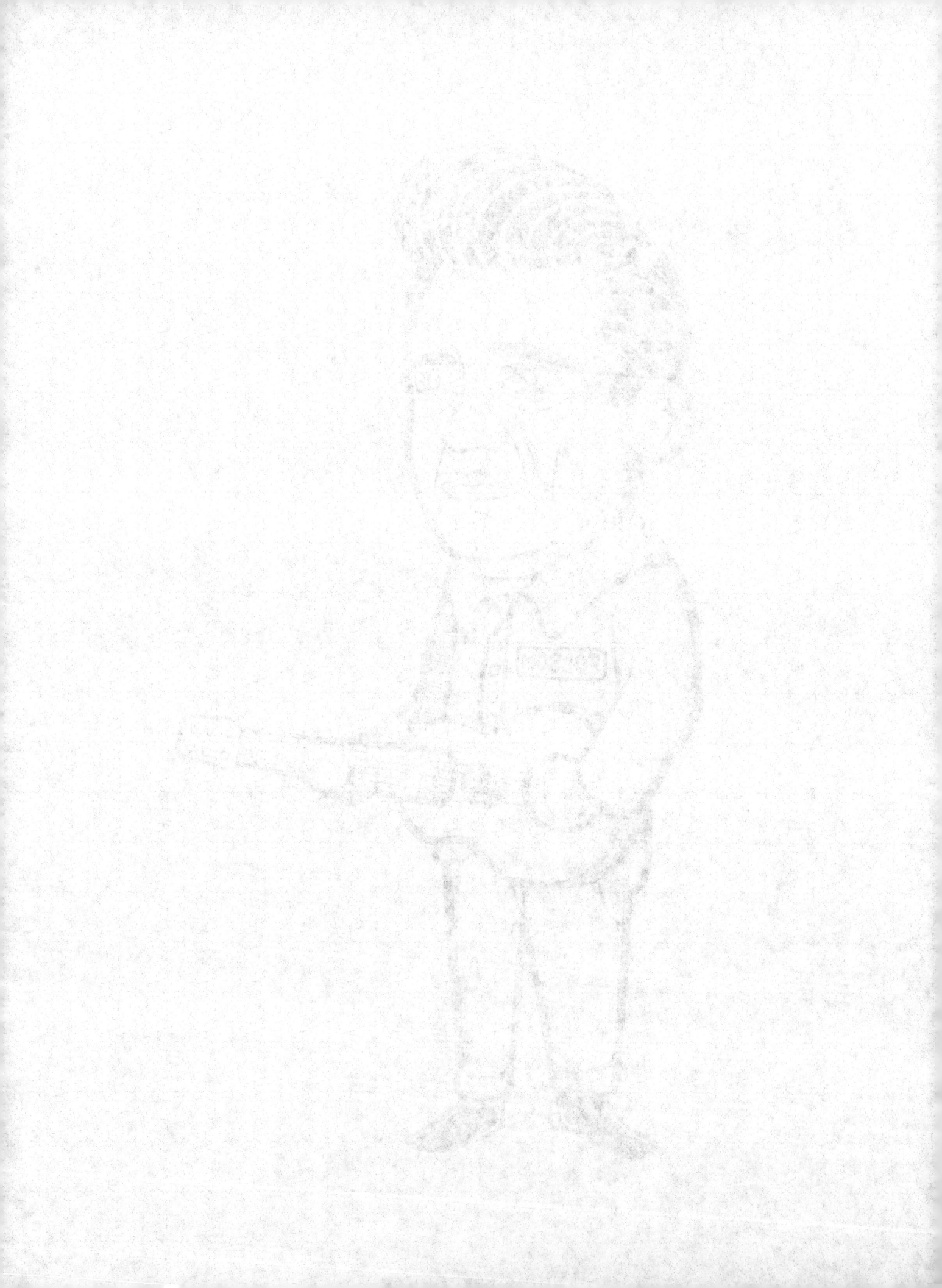

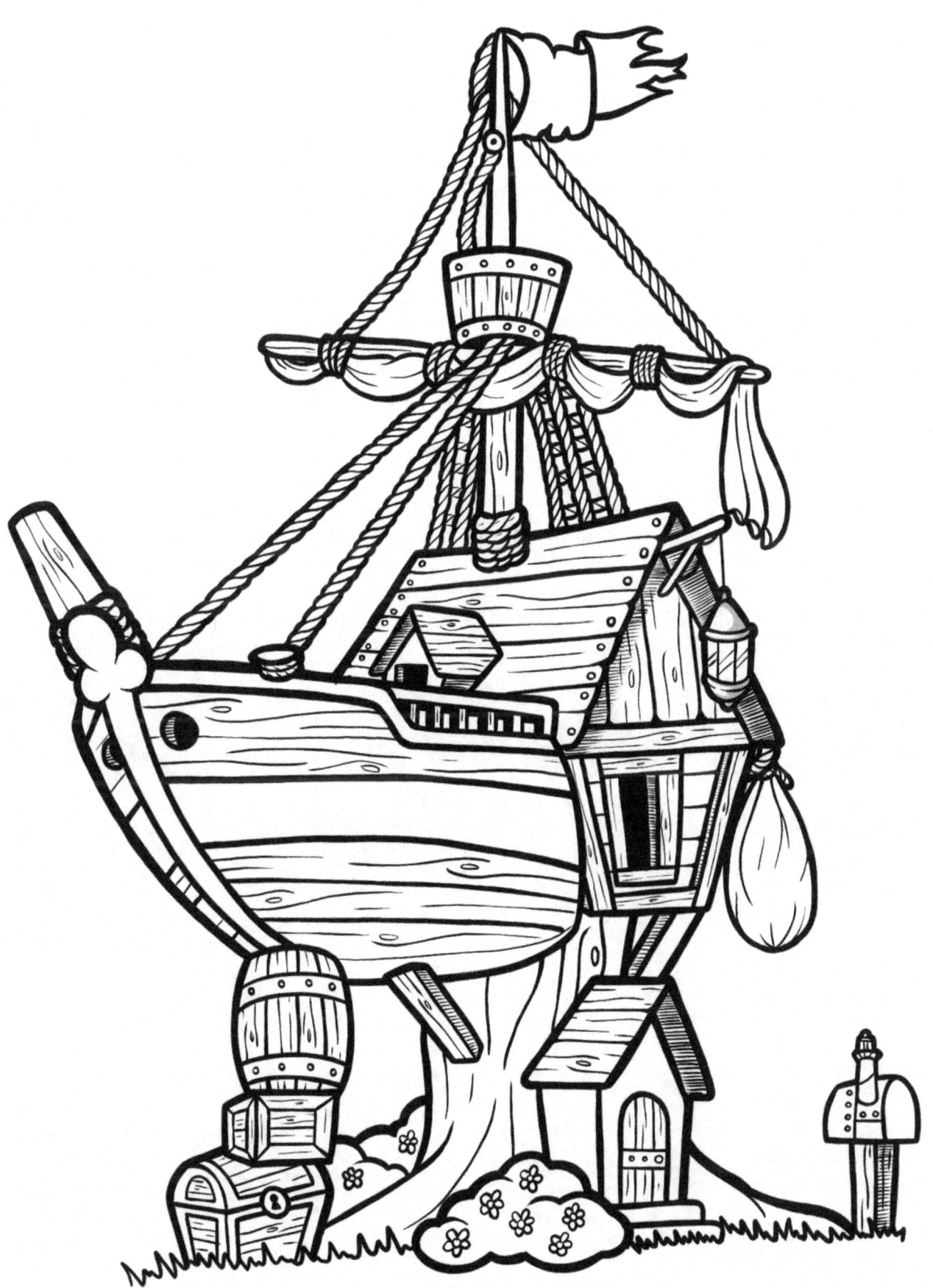

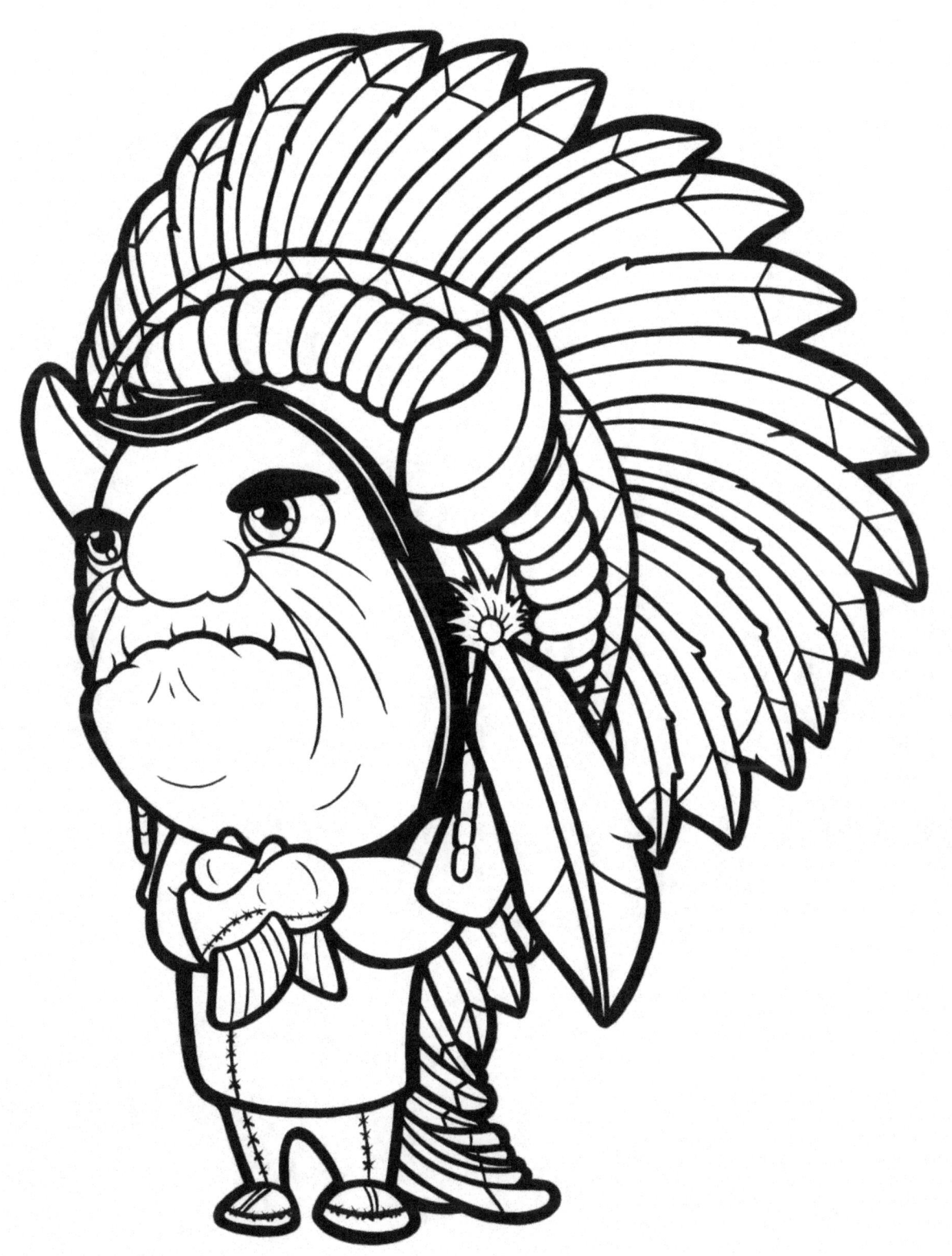

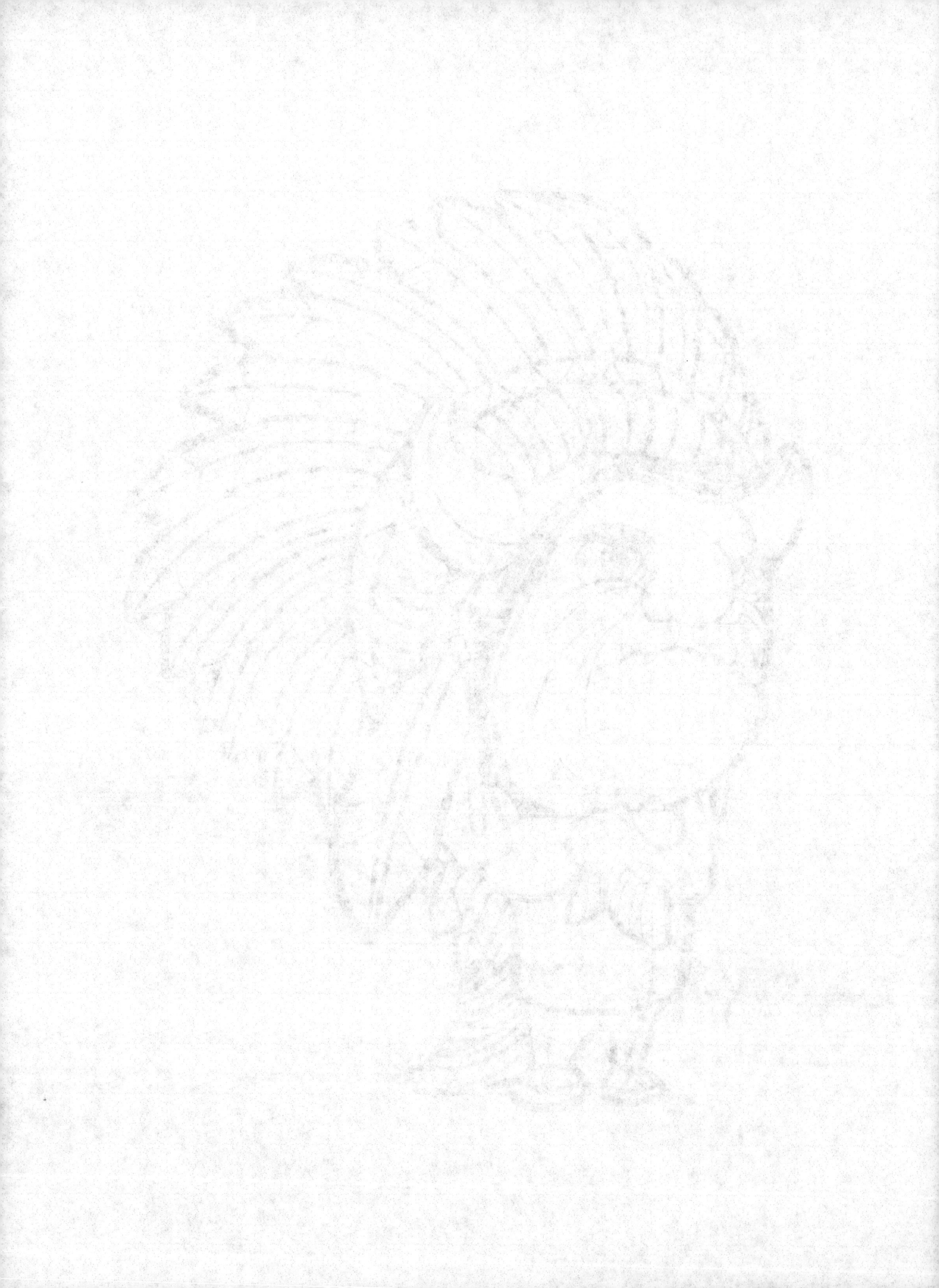

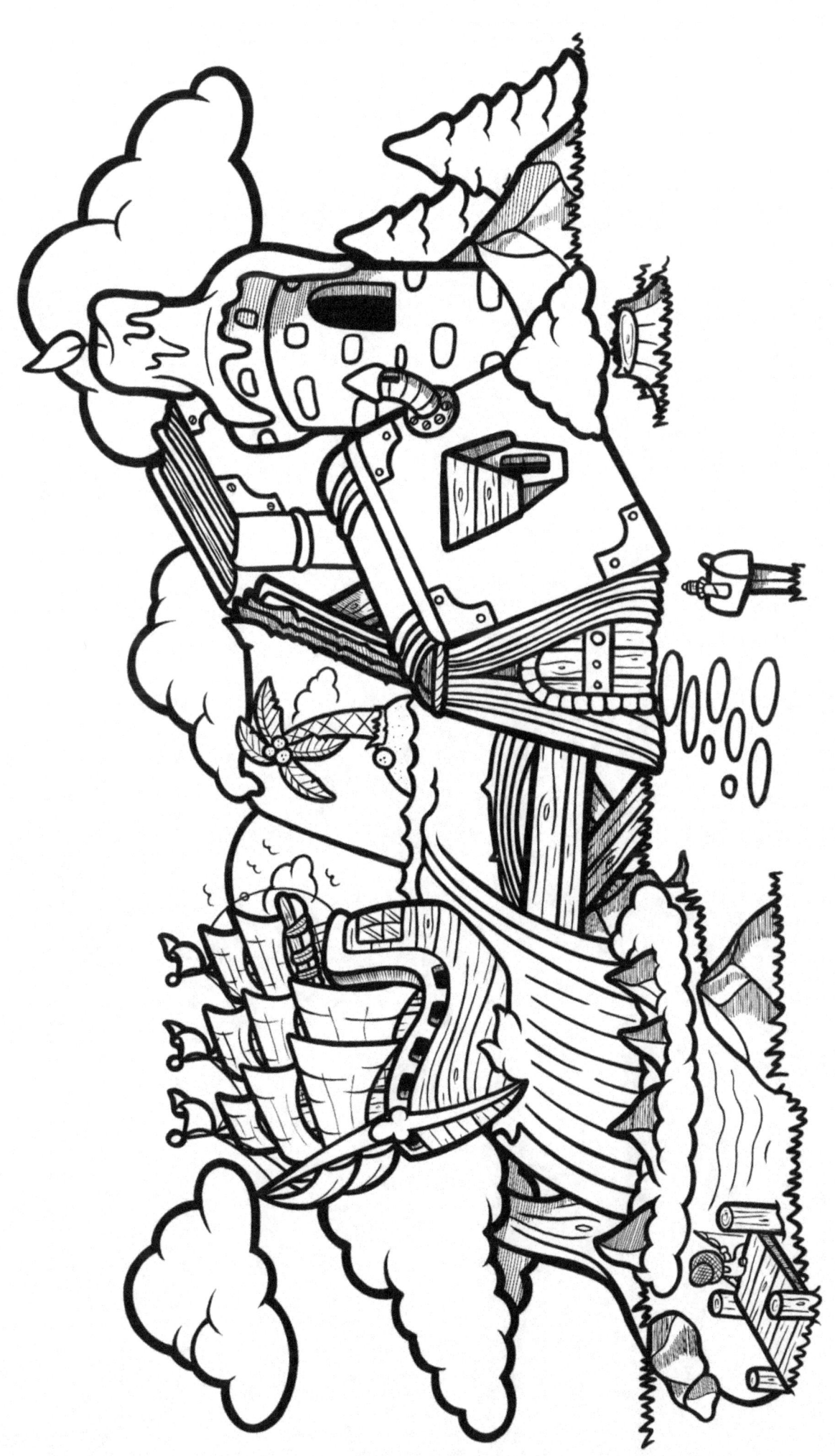

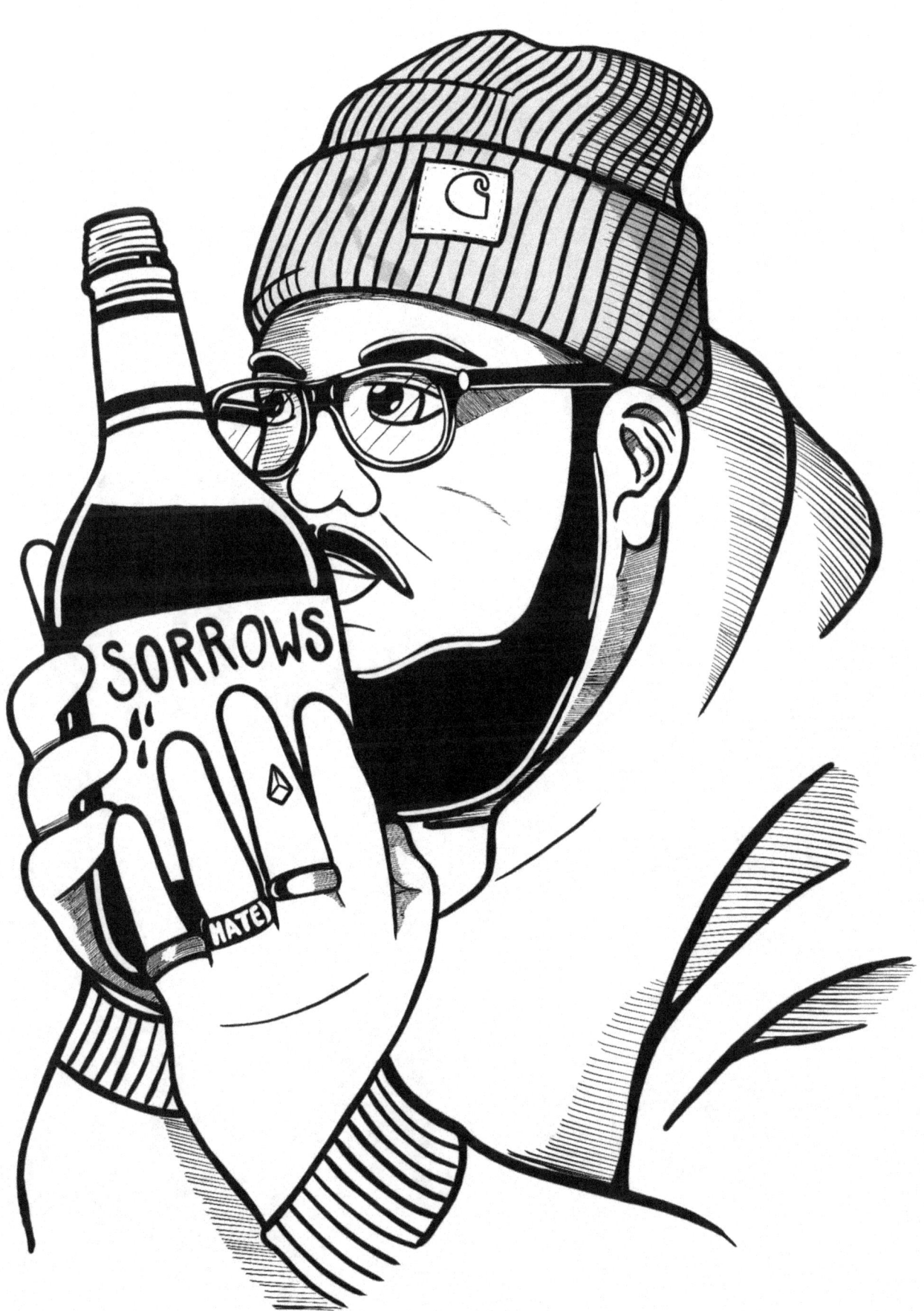

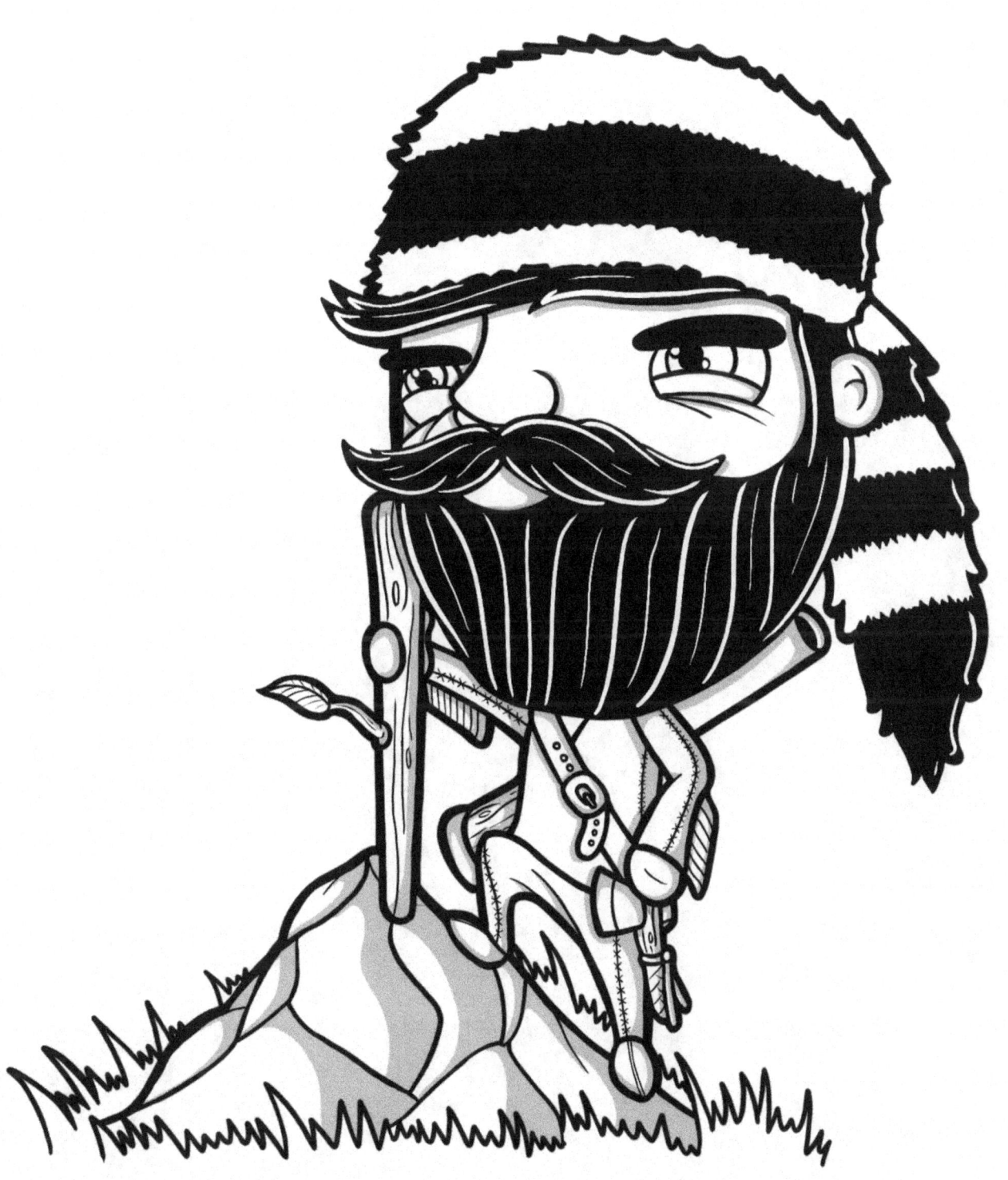

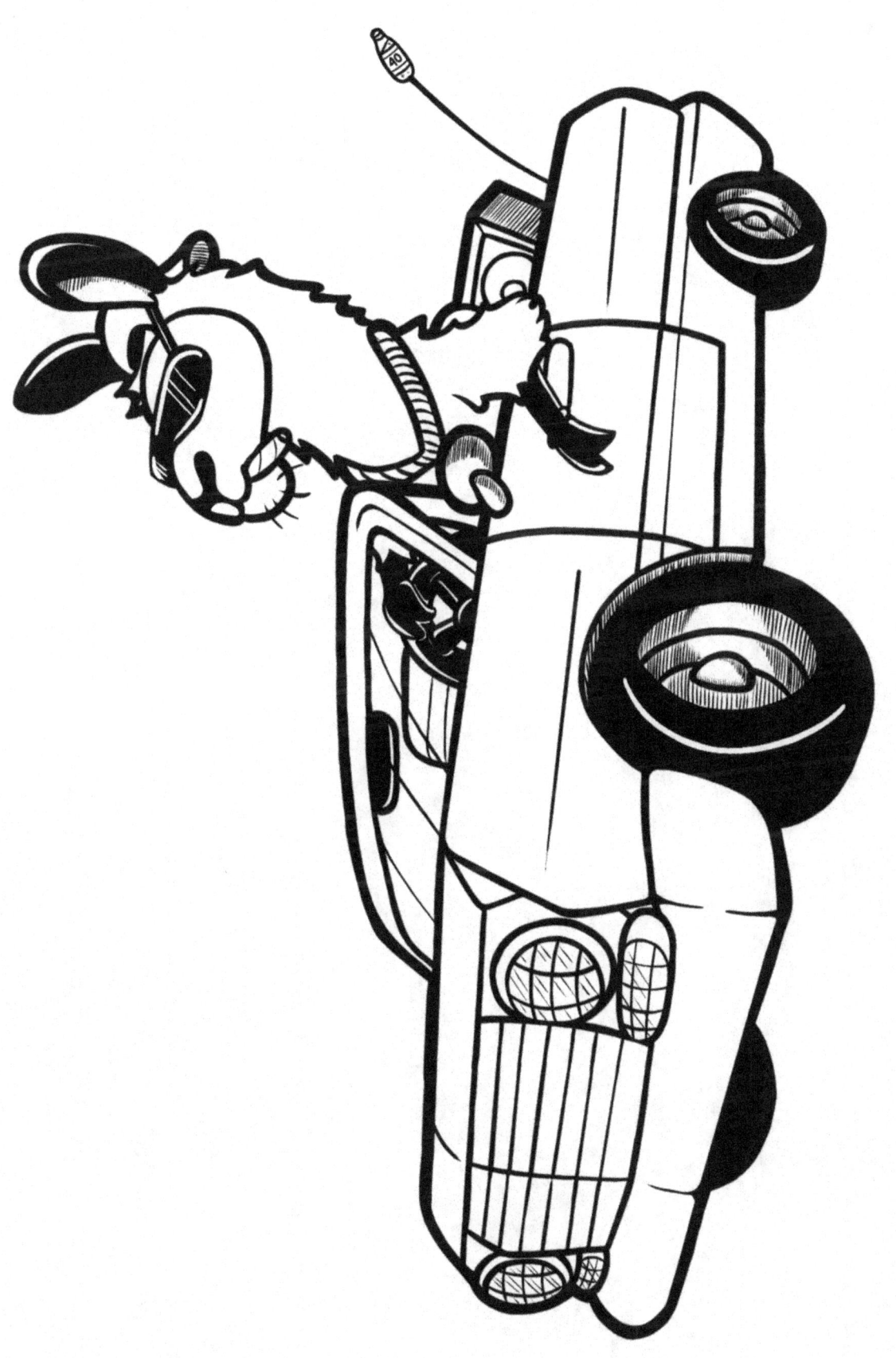

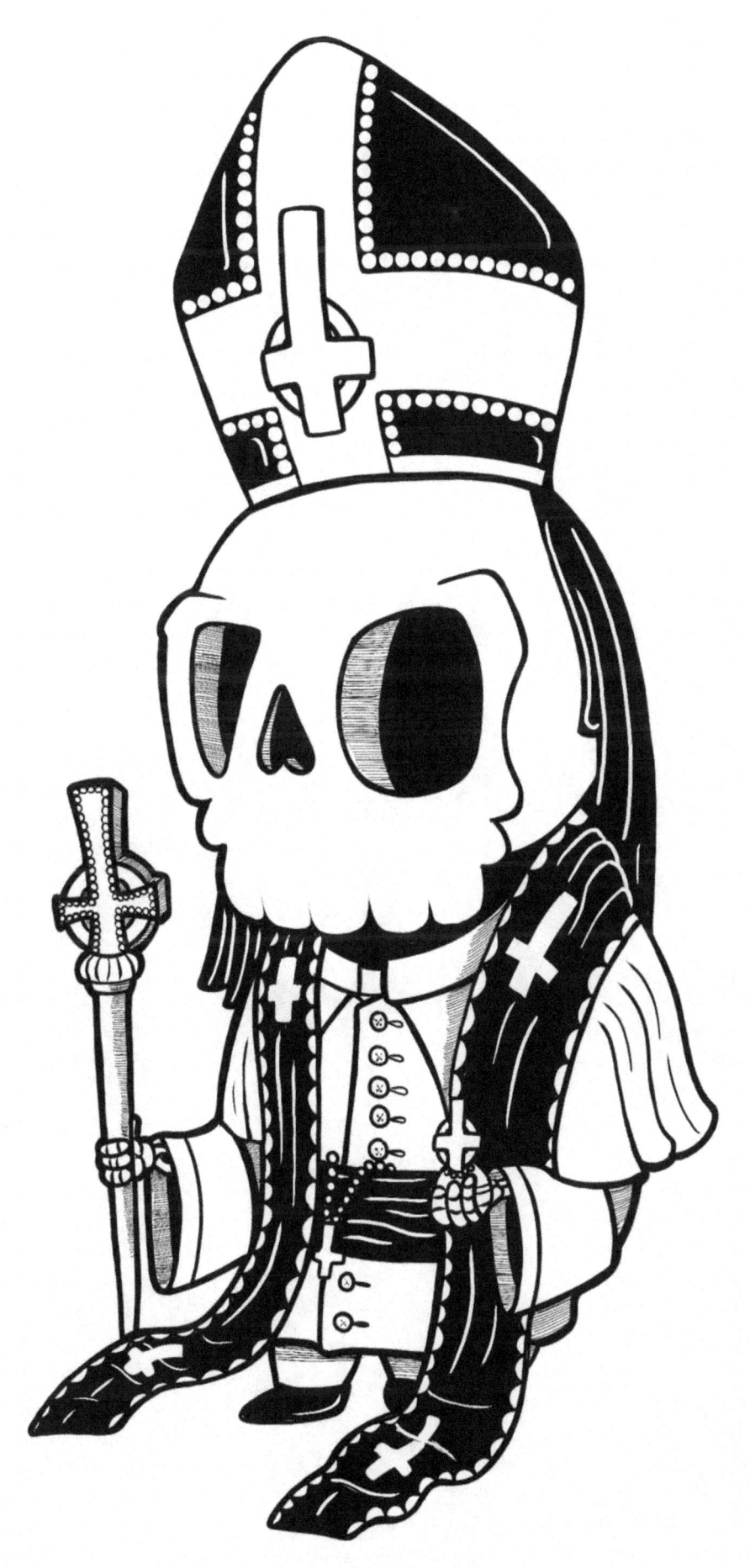

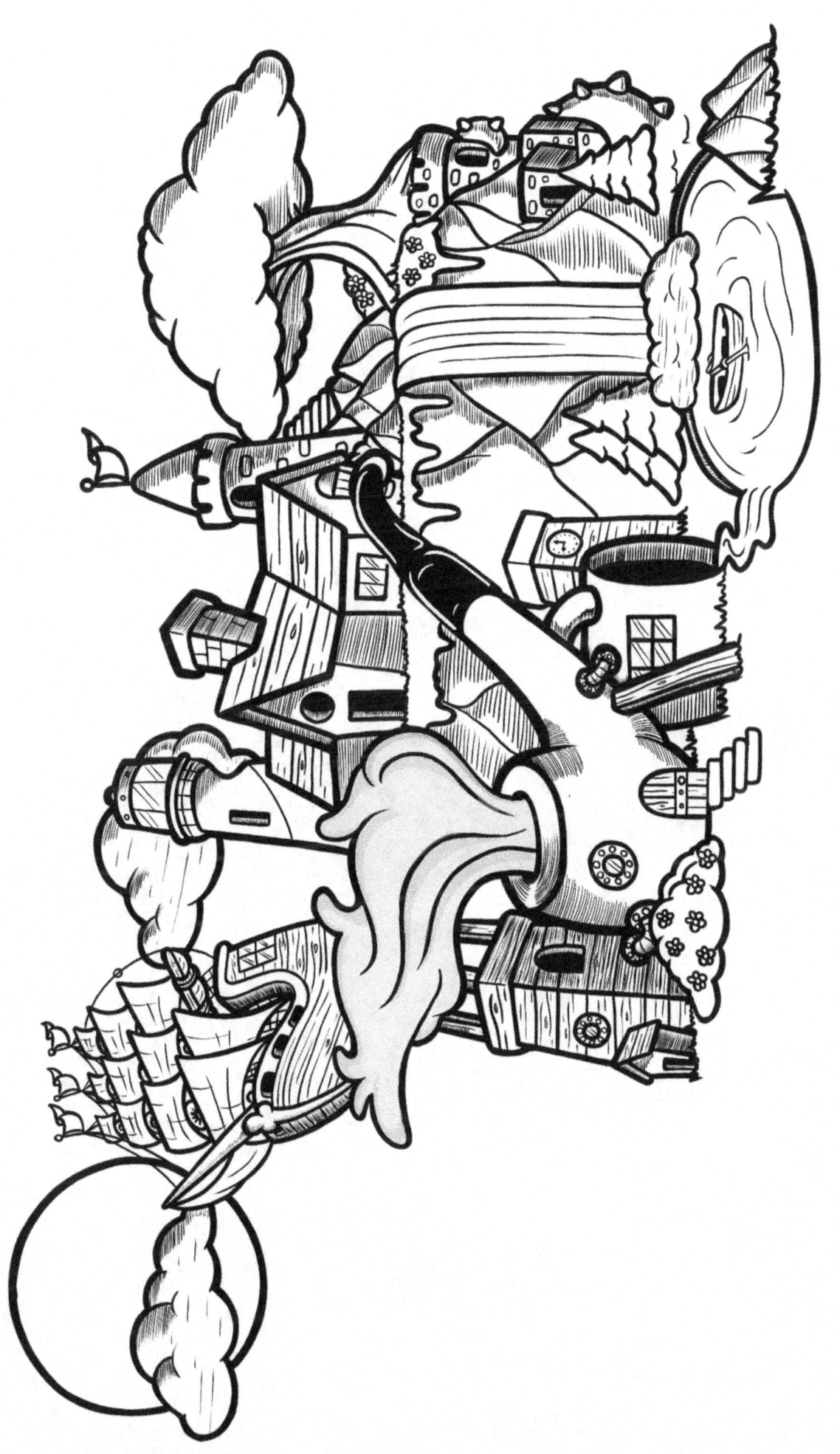

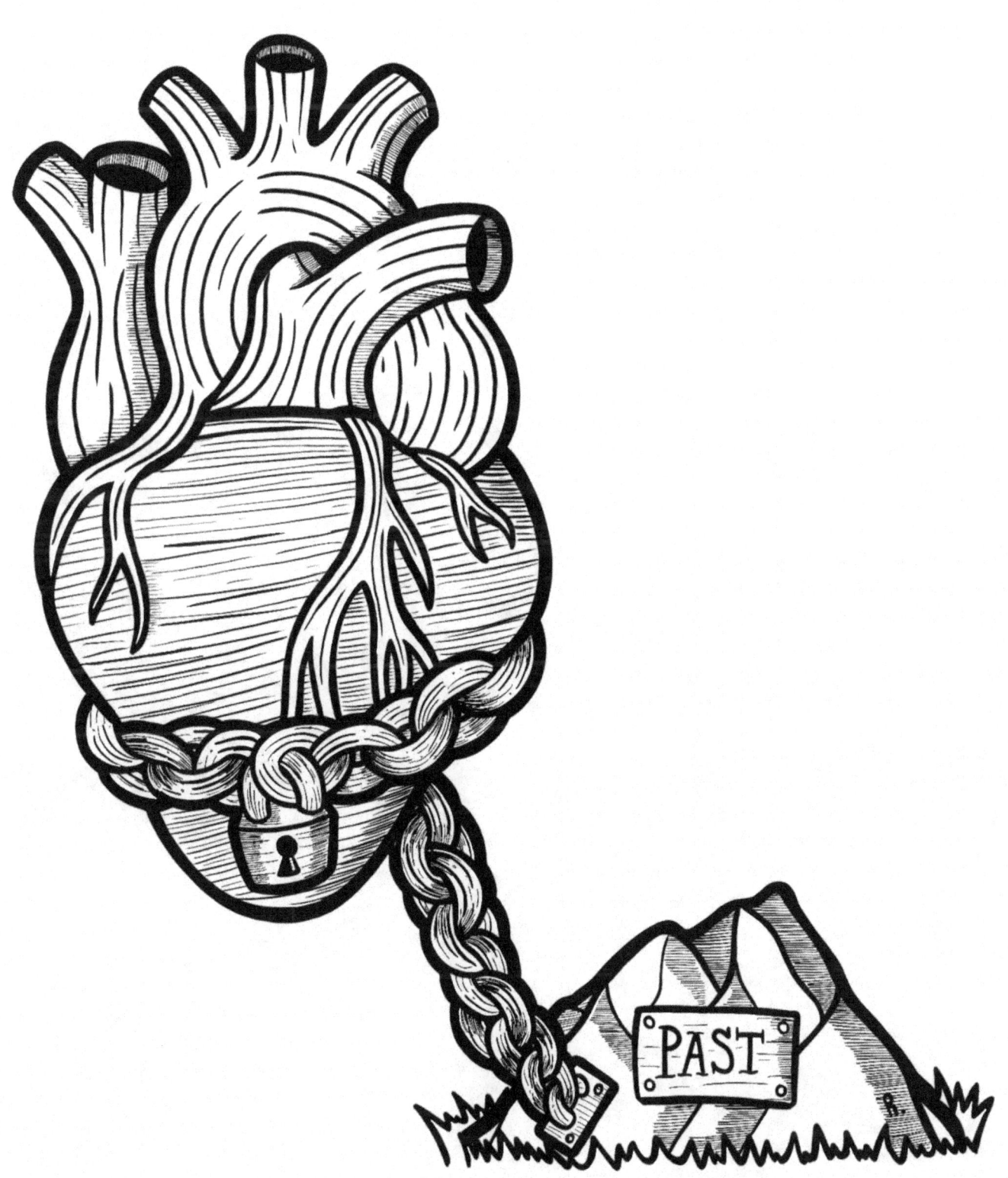

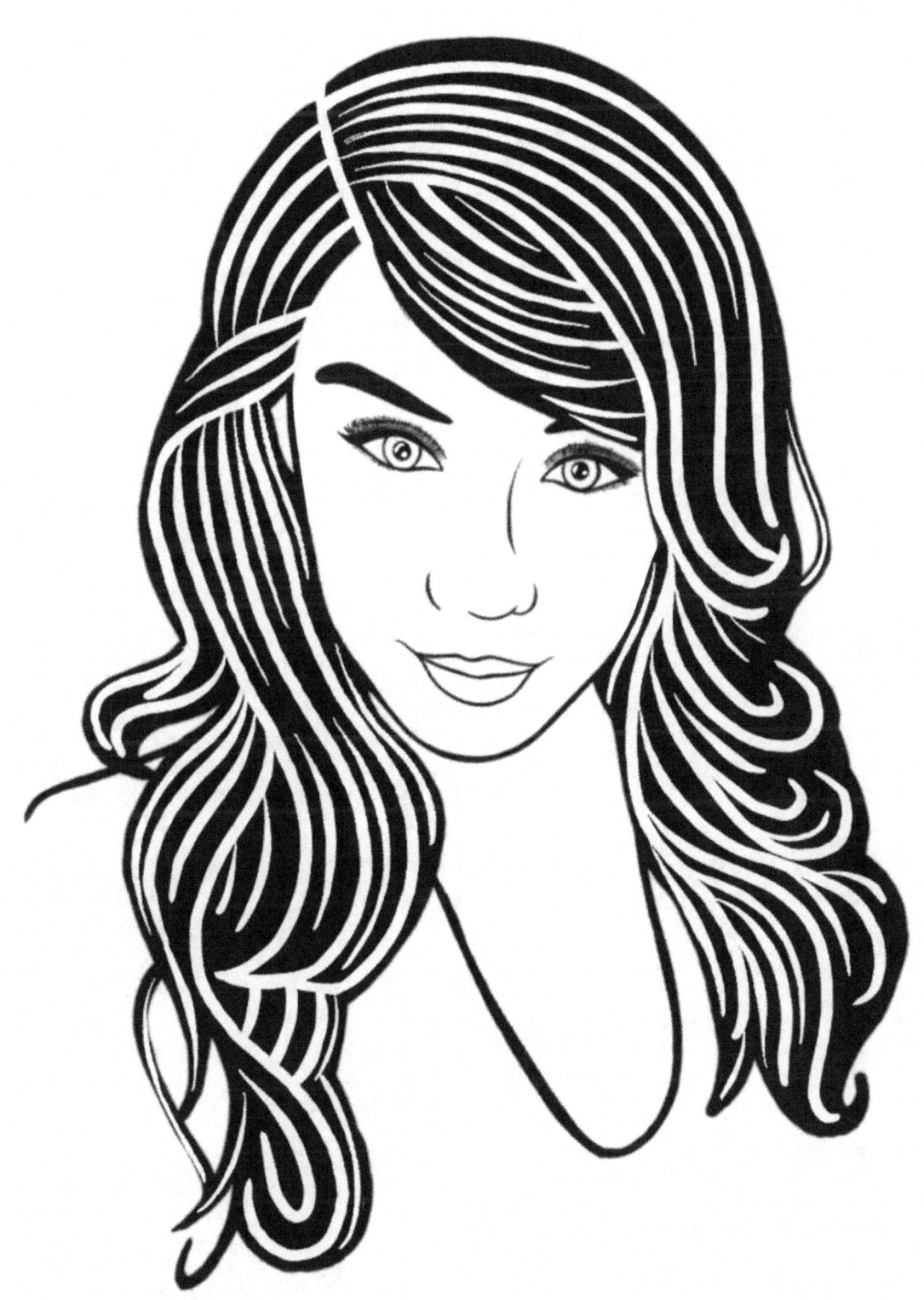

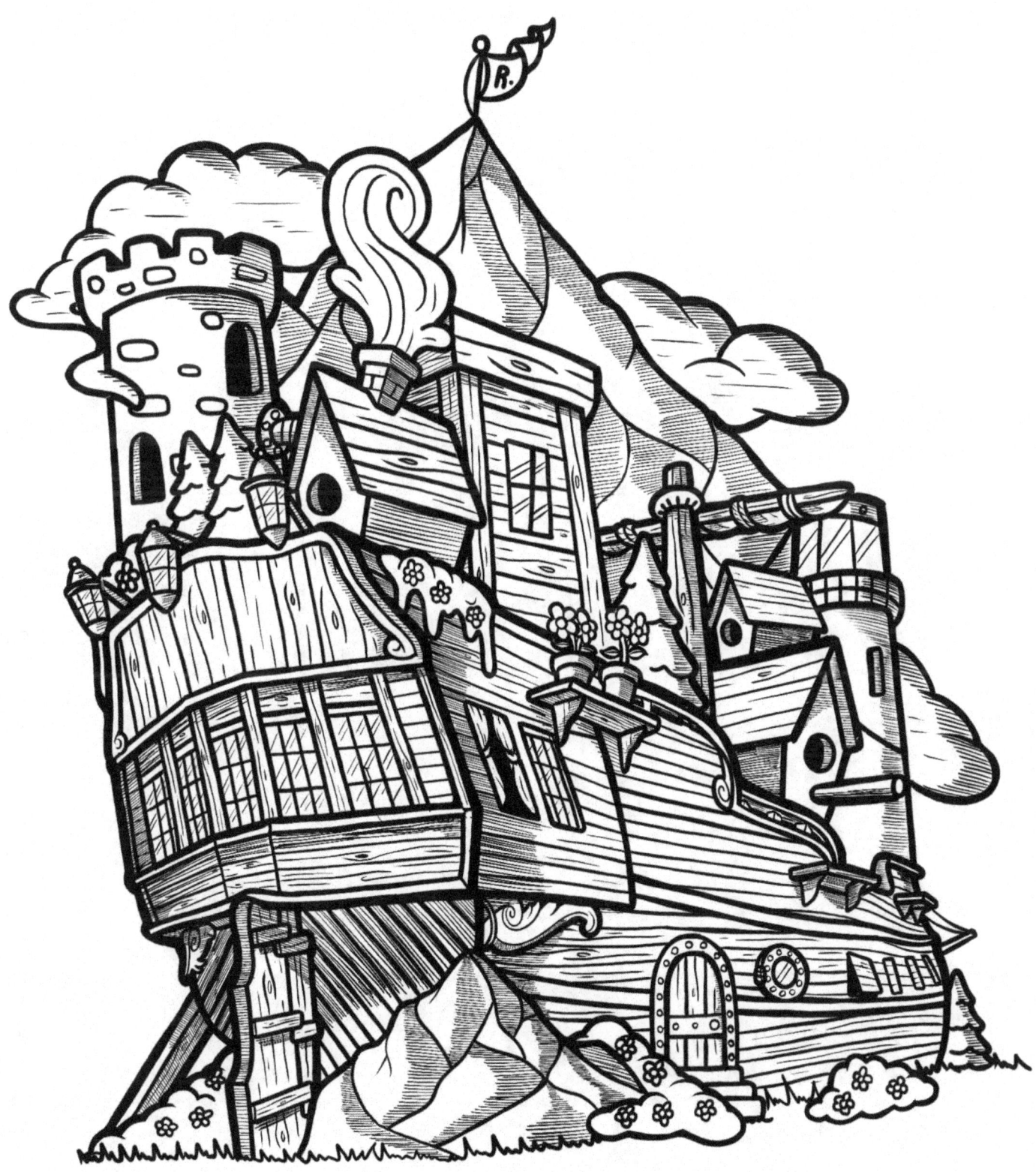

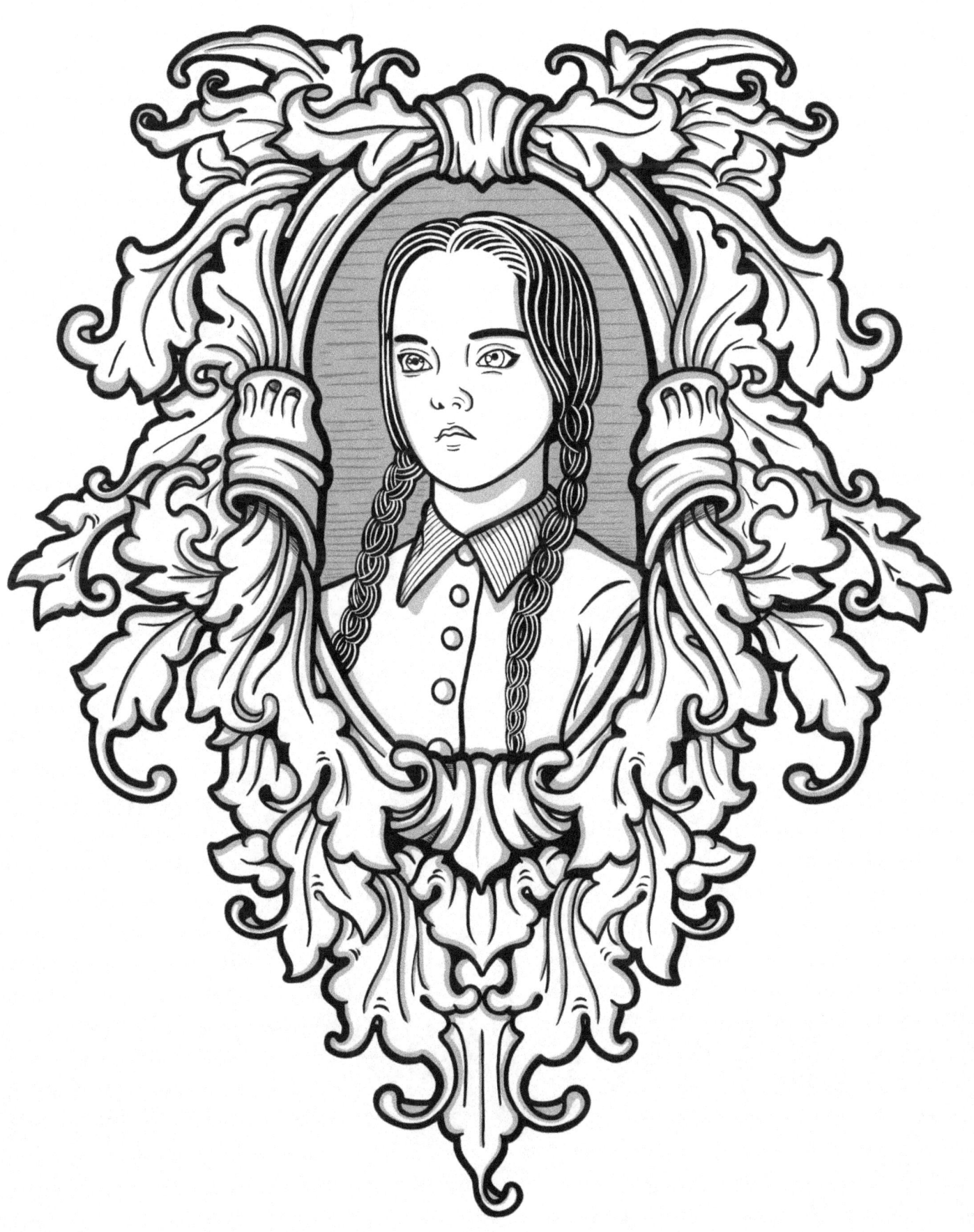

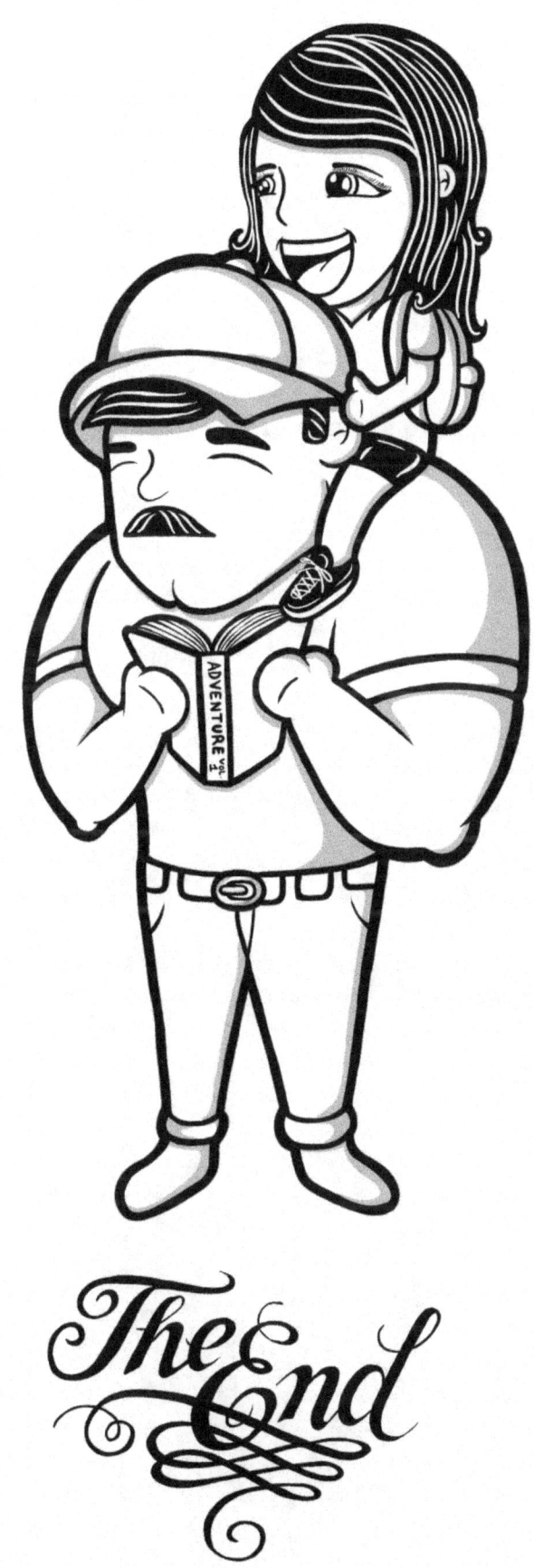

The End

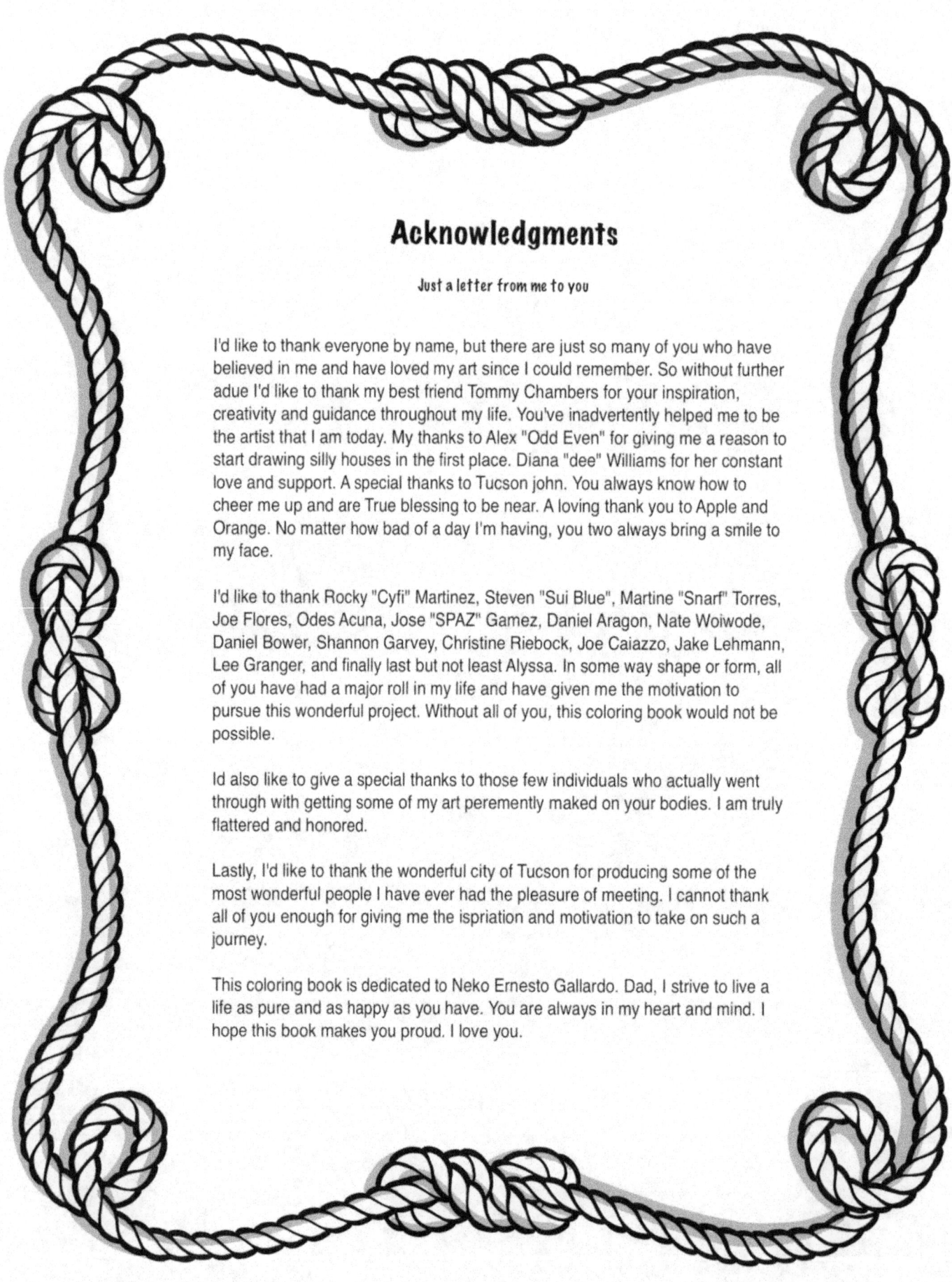

Acknowledgments

Just a letter from me to you

I'd like to thank everyone by name, but there are just so many of you who have believed in me and have loved my art since I could remember. So without further adue I'd like to thank my best friend Tommy Chambers for your inspiration, creativity and guidance throughout my life. You've inadvertently helped me to be the artist that I am today. My thanks to Alex "Odd Even" for giving me a reason to start drawing silly houses in the first place. Diana "dee" Williams for her constant love and support. A special thanks to Tucson john. You always know how to cheer me up and are True blessing to be near. A loving thank you to Apple and Orange. No matter how bad of a day I'm having, you two always bring a smile to my face.

I'd like to thank Rocky "Cyfi" Martinez, Steven "Sui Blue", Martine "Snarf" Torres, Joe Flores, Odes Acuna, Jose "SPAZ" Gamez, Daniel Aragon, Nate Woiwode, Daniel Bower, Shannon Garvey, Christine Riebock, Joe Caiazzo, Jake Lehmann, Lee Granger, and finally last but not least Alyssa. In some way shape or form, all of you have had a major roll in my life and have given me the motivation to pursue this wonderful project. Without all of you, this coloring book would not be possible.

Id also like to give a special thanks to those few individuals who actually went through with getting some of my art peremently maked on your bodies. I am truly flattered and honored.

Lastly, I'd like to thank the wonderful city of Tucson for producing some of the most wonderful people I have ever had the pleasure of meeting. I cannot thank all of you enough for giving me the ispriation and motivation to take on such a journey.

This coloring book is dedicated to Neko Ernesto Gallardo. Dad, I strive to live a life as pure and as happy as you have. You are always in my heart and mind. I hope this book makes you proud. I love you.